Bid Your Burdens *Goodbye*

An A-to-Z Guide to Letting Go of What Weighs You Down

Brenda Phegley

Inscript Books
A Division of Kingdom Christian Enterprises
PO Box 611
Bladensburg, MD 20710-0611

To my precious grandchildren

Lillian
Olivia
Caroline
Madelyn
Landon

"Every time I think of you, I give thanks to my God."
-Philippians 1:3 (NLT)

Contents

S

T

U

V

W

X

Y

Z

INTRODUCTION

*Y*ou may feel as if anxiety and worry are weighing you down, and help is nowhere to be found. Maybe doubt and despair are breaking your heart, and your life is falling apart. Or turmoil and tragedy are taking over your soul, and you wonder where you can go. That is when you should turn to God and bid your burdens goodbye!

God wants to free you from your heavy burdens. That is why He sent Jesus to the cross to take the weight of your sins with Him. You need to abandon your anxiety, depart from despair, and flee from fear. You must get rid of your guilt, pack away your pride, and walk away from your worries. The enemy tries to convince you that you must remain trapped under the heavy burdens of life, but Jesus tells you that He will set you free! He will help you escape from envy, oppose the onslaught of evil, and trade your turmoil for trust.

When you read *Bid Your Burdens Goodbye*, I pray that you will be encouraged by stories and Scriptures that will help you let go of your burdens. God's Word gives you practical advice on how you can clean out the clutter, quit your quest for more stuff, and zap your bad habits. When you jettison the junk in your life, you will be able to lighten your load with laughter, pray more and panic less, and zone in on what matters most. When you discover how to let go of what is weighing you down, then you can bid your burdens goodbye!

ABANDON YOUR ANXIETY

"Cast all your anxiety on him because he cares for you."

-1 Peter 5:7 (NIV)

A sense of uneasiness and dread begins creeping up on you. It causes you to fear, stress, and worry about minor or major events. You feel your heart begin to beat rapidly as anxiety refuses to loosen its stranglehold on you!

Everyone has feelings of anxiety at some point in their lives. What causes anxiety in one person may not cause anxiety in someone else. According to the National Institute of Mental Health, anxiety disorders are common, affecting 40 million people in America, with women being twice as likely to suffer from anxiety disorders as men. So, what can we do to prevent our anxiety from weighing us down? Sometimes, we cannot change our life circumstances. Natural disasters, terrorist attacks, and economic downturns are beyond our control; however, we can control how much time we spend with Jesus. Every moment in God's Word helps us deal with the chaos in the world. The chaos will still be there, but our outlook will be different. Reading the Bible will alleviate our anxiety when life is out of control. The Bible gives us many examples of people who had feelings of anxiety.

- King David was anointed by Samuel to be Israel's next king; however, Saul was still king, and he became jealous of David's growing popularity. Therefore, Saul began a vengeful quest to kill David, so David fled to the wilderness and lived as a fugitive, hiding out in caves to escape Saul. Without a doubt, David was filled with anxiety, but he cried out to God to help him in his distress because he remembered how God had comforted him in the past. "When anxiety was great within me, your consolation brought me joy" (Psalm 94:19 NIV).

- The prophet Elijah was threatened by the evil Queen Jezebel after his dramatic victory over the prophets of Baal at Mount Carmel. Jezebel sent a messenger who told Elijah that Jezebel planned to kill him because he had killed her prophets. This information caused Elijah to feel anxious and desperate, so he fled into the wilderness. His anxiety became so intense that he wanted to die. However, God sent an angel to minister to Elijah by providing him with food and water to strengthen him. "Then he lay down and slept under the broom tree. But as he was sleeping, an angel touched him and told him, 'Get up and eat!'" (1 Kings 19:5 NLT).

- When Martha was hosting a dinner for Jesus, she became so anxious about being the perfect hostess that she became upset with Jesus. Why? Because her sister Mary was not helping; she was listening to Jesus teach. Jesus told Martha, "Martha, you are anxious and troubled about many things. But one thing is needed. And Mary has chosen the good part, which shall not be taken from her" (Luke 10:41-42 MEV). Martha was so worried about having everything perfect for Jesus that she missed the main thing—Jesus was at her home.

Jesus is at our homes every day, and He is ready to take our anxiety away! We simply need to abandon our anxiety and cast our cares upon Jesus! He gives us rest for our anxious hearts, and His tremendous love will never depart!

When you feel that anxiety is weighing you down,
You should try to smile—not frown.
Because Jesus will deliver you from fear,
And reassure you that help is near.
You must remember to cast your cares upon Him,
In order for Jesus' blessings to begin.
When anxiety causes you to feel distressed,
Call upon Jesus for His perfect rest.

AIM FOR CONTENTMENT

"I am not saying this because I am in need, for I have learned to be content whatever the circumstances."

-Philippians 4:11 (NIV)

How can we learn to be content? It is really quite simple! Strive to live with less rather than desiring more; give things away rather than accumulating more. Appreciate what you have instead of resenting what you do not have. We become content when we realize that God has given us everything we need, rather than everything we want. If you have ever taken three-year-old children to a toy store, they cry out that they want everything they see. We may not act like three-year-olds; however, we simply purchase unnecessary items, and then we become burdened by all of our junk! To be content, we must resist the constant bombardment of advertisers trying to convince us that our lives will become magically better once we purchase their products.

Many people will never appreciate what they have if they depend upon their possessions to make them happy. The apostle Paul learned to be content and appreciate what he had. "I know what it is to be in need, and I know what it is to have plenty. I have learned the secret of being content in any and every situation, whether well fed or hungry, whether living in plenty or in want" (Philippians

4:12 NIV). Paul was beaten, whipped, stoned, shipwrecked, tossed into the sea, harassed by enemies, and betrayed by false believers, but he was content. Paul realized that Christ supplied him with contentment, no matter what circumstances he faced.

If we become attached to the things of this world, we will constantly be in a state of discontent. If we examine the life of Helen Lemmel, we find a woman who learned to focus on Jesus for contentment in life. Helen Lemmel (1863-1961) was born in England, and her family moved to the United States when Helen was twelve years old. Helen became a talented singer, and she traveled throughout the country singing at many venues. Then she decided to move to Germany to improve her singing abilities, and in 1907, she married a wealthy man. She was living a wonderful life, but tragedy struck when she became blind, and her husband abandoned her. Even though she was destitute, she believed that her faith in Christ would sustain her. She learned to turn her eyes upon Jesus, instead of the things of this world. Her positive mindset inspired her to write her now-famous hymn, "Turn Your Eyes Upon Jesus."[1]

> O Soul, are you weary and troubled?
> No light in the darkness you see:
> There's light for a look at the Savior,
> And life more abundant and free!
> Turn your eyes upon Jesus,
> Look full in His wonderful face,
> And the things of earth will grow strangely dim,
> In the light of His glory and grace.[2]

The only way we will find contentment is to turn our eyes upon Jesus! If we turn our eyes upon what the world offers, we will always be seeking more, and we will never be satisfied!

Contentment should be our aim,
Not money, possessions, or fame.
If we quit desiring more and learn to live with less,
We will find our lives will be blessed.
Aiming for contentment makes us free,
And shows us how happy our lives can be.
When we learn that God has supplied every need,
Then our hearts will be content indeed!

AVOID TEMPTATIONS AND TRAPS

"Those who want to get rich fall into temptation and a trap and into many foolish and harmful desires that plunge people into ruin and destruction."

-1 Timothy 6:9 (NIV)

*M*any people believe that money brings happiness. Unfortunately, some people who seek riches have been lured into temptations and traps that lead to destruction. Why is the quest for money so alluring? Why are people willing to risk their lives simply to get rich?

A classic example of the malignant effects of avarice is narrated by the greedy Pardoner in *The Canterbury Tales* by Geoffrey Chaucer. The story is set in a time period when a plague was taking the lives of many people, so three young men decide that they want to prevent the loss of more lives; therefore, they venture out on a quest to find "Death" so they can kill him. They begin their journey, and they meet an old man who tells them that they will find Death under a tree. So, the young men go to the tree, and instead of finding Death, they are pleasantly surprised to find eight bushel-baskets of gold. They realize that they cannot carry the gold away during the day without someone suspecting them of being thieves.

Therefore, they decide that they will wait until dark. Because they are hungry and thirsty, they decide that one of the young men must go into town to get food and drinks. As soon as this young man leaves, the other two men decide that they will kill him when he returns, so they can have all of the gold themselves. Meanwhile, the young man who went into town decides to buy poison to place in the drinks for the other two men, so he can have all of the gold himself. When he returns to the two men, they kill him, and then they celebrate by drinking the poisoned drinks. Just as the old man had promised the young men, they found Death under a tree. If the young men had been content to share the gold and not been greedy, they could have enjoyed their wealth! The love of money caused the demise of these young men. "For the love of money is a root of all kinds of evil. Some people, eager for money, have wandered from the faith and pierced themselves with many griefs" (1 Timothy 6:10 NIV).

It is the "love of money" that causes people to lie, steal, cheat, gamble, embezzle, and even murder. We should not fall into the trap of allowing money to control us. Some people have fallen into the trap of searching for buried treasure, and they have lost everything during their quest. In 2010, Forrest Fenn (1930-2020) buried a treasure chest somewhere north of Santa Fe and south of Canada in the Rocky Mountains. The chest contained gold coins, gems, and jewelry worth over $1 million. Fenn wrote a poem that gave clues to the location of the buried treasure. Thousands of people searched for the treasure, with many people wasting years of their lives and thousands of dollars on the quest. Tragically, five people died during their search. The treasure was finally discovered in 2020.[1] Was losing one's life worth the price of a buried treasure? "Don't wear yourself out trying to get rich; be wise enough to control yourself" (Proverbs 23:4 NCV). We should not waste our lives looking for a treasure buried in the ground because our treasure has been found! Jesus will keep us from falling into temptations and traps!

The love of money can be our downfall
When we sell our souls and lose it all.
If we fall into the trap of greed,
We fail to realize what we truly need.
If we waste our lives on the money quest,
We forfeit what God has given us—His best.
When the love of money is our ultimate goal,
We gain the whole world but lose our soul.

BELIEVE IN THE GOODNESS OF GOD

"The Lord is good to everyone; he is merciful to all he has made."

-Psalm 145:9 (NCV)

God always acts in accordance with what is right, true, and good. Goodness is part of God's nature. The evil in the world did not come from God, and God did not create evil. We must remember that God does not burden us with evil—Satan does this!

We may mistakenly believe that if we are experiencing hardship, trouble, sickness, or the death of a loved one that God is not good. If He was good, then bad things would not happen—at least not to "good" people. However, God's goodness is extended to everyone. This does not mean that we are immune to pain in our lives; it simply means that we must always remember that this life is only temporary. One day, we will bask in God's goodness all the time. There will be no more pain and suffering!

Sometimes, God uses adversity in people's lives in order to allow them to become a blessing to others. The life of Lina Sandell (1832-1903) is a reminder of this truth. Lina was stricken with an illness, causing partial paralysis when she was young. Her doctors believed her chance of recovery was hopeless; however, her parents believed in God's goodness and healing power. Lina experienced complete healing from her illness when she was twelve years old.

After this miracle, Lina began writing poetry, expressing her gratitude to God. Then tragedy struck her life again when she was twenty-six years old. She was with her father on a boat trip across Lake Vättern in Sweden, and her father fell overboard and drowned. Even though she witnessed this tragedy, she still believed in God's goodness and was inspired to write a poem titled "Day by Day," which became a well-known hymn. The words of the hymn, "He, whose heart is kind beyond all measure, gives into each day what He deems best," focus on God's goodness every day. Lina Sandell eventually wrote more than 650 hymns, and she became Sweden's most celebrated author of gospel hymns. The famous opera singer, Jenny Lind, known as the "Swedish Nightingale," sang many of Lina's hymns, and her hymns helped many people believe in the goodness of God.[1]

Another person who believed in the goodness of God despite suffering adversity was Joseph Scriven (1819-1886). On the day before Joseph's wedding, his fiancée died in a drowning accident. After this tragedy, Joseph moved from Ireland to Canada, where he fell in love again. Weeks before his wedding, his fiancée became ill and died. Joseph was only twenty-five years old. Years later, when Joseph's mother became ill, he wrote her a poem titled, "What a Friend We Have in Jesus." Joseph definitely believed in the goodness of God despite suffering tremendous loss in his life. He stated that God hears all of our prayers: "What a friend we have in Jesus, all our sins and griefs to bear. What a privilege to carry everything to God in prayer."[2]

We can choose to be bitter or to be blessed. We can choose to fret about the bad or focus on the good. We can choose to drown in our despair or triumph over our tragedies. But whatever we choose, we must know that God's goodness will always prevail. His goodness will always surround us, uplift us, and bless us. "Examine and see how good the Lord is. Happy is the person who trusts in him" (Psalm 34:8 NCV).

God's goodness surrounds us every day,
We simply need to seek His blessings along the way.
We will all experience tragedy and pain,
But God's goodness will remain.
When we focus on suffering and adversity,
Then God's goodness we fail to see.
If we seek the good instead of the bad,
Then our lives will be happy—not sad!

BRIGHTEN SOMEONE'S DAY

"Therefore encourage one another and build each other up, just as in fact you are doing."

-1 Thessalonians 5:11 (NIV)

How do you feel when you receive a simple compliment, a thoughtful card, or an unexpected gift? You feel fantastic! It is so easy to brighten someone's day. Without encouragement, life would feel pointless and burdensome. Without encouragement, we may feel unloved because feeling valued and appreciated are important to everyone. When I was a college professor, I would always find something positive to write on every student's paper. Because of my positive comments, oftentimes, the students who were not the "best" students would improve on their next writing assignments.

We never know how much our encouragement will help other people. During the American Revolutionary War, Martha Washington joined her husband, George, at his winter encampment. Martha's presence at the camp encouraged her husband and also boosted the camp morale. Martha became good friends with the wives of other officers, and they encouraged each other by talking, singing, and doing needlework together. Martha also comforted sick and wounded soldiers, and she sponsored social activities that improved camp morale.[1]

Another woman who made an impact on others' lives with her acts of encouragement was Mary Ann Bickerdyke (1817-1901). During the American Civil War, Mary Ann Bickerdyke volunteered as a nurse. She left her family to help distribute supplies at a makeshift army hospital in Cairo, Illinois. Upon arrival at the hospital, she was appalled by the unsanitary conditions, so she began cleaning, cooking, and caring for the wounded soldiers. After the fall of Fort Donelson in 1862, Bickerdyke searched the battlefield for wounded soldiers. She then followed General Grant's army down the Mississippi River, setting up hospitals along the way. Under Bickerdyke's supervision, approximately 300 field hospitals were built with the assistance of U.S. Sanitary Commission agents. Bickerdyke became known as "Mother" Bickerdyke among the sick and wounded soldiers because of her love and compassion. Bickerdyke's acts of encouragement lifted the spirits of the soldiers.[2]

We should all try to brighten someone's day with simple acts of encouragement. A simple smile, a caring compliment, or a thoughtful "thank-you" do not take much effort, but these things may be what someone needs. When we have the love of Jesus in our hearts, then encouraging others is doing our part. When we make an effort to be the bright spot in someone's day, then we show them that encouragement is on the way! In a world that is often centered on "self," it is reassuring to think of ways to encourage someone else! "Do not be interested only in your own life, but be interested in the lives of others" (Philippians 2:4 NCV).

It is so easy to brighten someone's day,
In everything you do and say.
You never know the burdens someone may bear,
So send a card to show you care.
A word of encouragement from a friend
May be what it takes for a heart to mend.
A simple smile on your face
Will spread love and joy in every place.

Build on a Firm Foundation

"And everyone who hears these words of mine and does not do them will be like a foolish man who built his house on the sand. And the rain fell, and the floods came, and the winds blew and beat against that house, and it fell, and great was the fall of it."

-Matthew 7:26-27 (ESV)

What happens when a strong foundation is not used for a building? It collapses! The Champlain Towers condominium in Surfside, Florida, collapsed on June 24, 2021, killing 98 people and injuring many others. This was one of the deadliest structural disasters in American history. According to researchers from Florida International University, the Champlain Towers had been sinking at a steady rate for years because it was built on reclaimed wetlands.[1]

A foundation is the basis or groundwork of something. If you do not build on a good foundation, you will be burdened with repairing a faulty foundation in the future. When my husband and I were building our house, we spent many weeks pouring the concrete and laying the concrete blocks for the basement of our house. It was a lot of hard work, but it was necessary to invest in a strong foundation. The foundation supports your home and bears the weight.

Without a solid base underneath, your house will suffer damage and possibly fall down. Without a proper foundation, a building or structure can shift, crack, or even collapse, resulting in costly repairs, injuries, or loss of life.

Just as we should have a strong foundation for a building, we must choose a strong foundation for our lives. If we build our lives upon temporary things, such as power, prestige, or possessions, we will not have a solid foundation, because these things can easily be taken away from us. If we build our lives upon the opinions and false truths of the world, we will have a foundation that is unstable, unreliable, and unpredictable. However, if we build our lives upon the solid rock of Christ, our lives will be secure.

When life is calm, our foundation does not seem important; however, when the storms of life assail us, our foundation is tested. We must make sure that our lives are built upon the solid rock of Christ, because all other ground is sinking sand! When we think of "sinking sand," we may envision a movie scene where a character falls into a pit of quicksand and is quickly swallowed up! Typically, people do not sink suddenly into quicksand; however, when people panic, they may sink deeper into the murky mire. Because quicksand can occur almost anywhere where water is located, we must watch out for it.

In 2019, two people were hiking in Zion National Park, and one of the hikers stepped into quicksand and was trapped for hours in freezing conditions while his girlfriend went looking for help. After ten hours, she returned, and it took rescuers two hours to free him from the quicksand.[2] Sometimes in life, we may think we have a firm foundation, but the unexpected can occur. When it does, we can count on God to rescue us and place us on a firm foundation. "He lifted me out of the slimy pit, out of the mud and mire; he set my feet on a rock and gave me a firm place to stand" (Psalm 40:2 NIV).

When life throws you in the mud and mire,
You may feel that your situation is dire.
When you build your life upon faulty ground,
You find that troubles and tragedies abound.
So remember that the solid rock of Christ will endure;
It is the only foundation that is secure.
When you build upon the only foundation that will last;
Your life will remain steadfast.

CLEAN OUT THE CLUTTER

"A time to search and a time to give up, a time to keep and a time to throw away."

-Ecclesiastes 3:6 (NIV)

If you were to come to my house, you would find that I do not like clutter! I have always enjoyed cleaning out closets and drawers and discarding unnecessary items. When I clean people's homes, I usually throw away or donate many items that create clutter.

Why is clutter a problem? It may gradually develop into hoarding. According to the Mayo Clinic, problems with hoarding develop gradually over time when people get and keep too many things that they do not need. Hoarders are reluctant to throw away items, regardless of their actual value, and eventually, hoarders cannot use rooms in their homes because of all the clutter covering the floors. This clutter can negatively impact a hoarder's life for the following reasons:

- Clutter can be dangerous because it can block doors, cause trip hazards, and result in choking hazards for small children. Piles of old mail, newspapers, and magazines are a fire hazard, especially if they cover outlets or are near space heaters.
- Clutter can cause physical problems because of the buildup of dust, dirt, and mold. Stacks of cardboard boxes can harbor brown recluse spiders, which are poisonous.

22

- Clutter may affect relationships because family members may be embarrassed to invite friends to their homes. If couches and chairs are filled with boxes, there is nowhere for people to sit.
- Clutter may result in unhealthy eating patterns if kitchen tables do not have any space for family meals. When meals are not eaten at the kitchen table, unhealthy eating habits can develop.
- Clutter can also result in mental health issues because messy homes make people feel overwhelmed and stressed. People may feel anxiety because they cannot find important items, which may cause them to always be late for school, work, or events.

The most significant problem with clutter is that it burdens us with the things of this world, which are insignificant. Instead of focusing on things of the spirit, we waste time sifting through piles of junk! "Think about the things of heaven, not the things of earth" (Colossians 3:2 NLT). We should not let our clutter rob us of our precious time, which is what it does. Donating unwanted items frees us, while accumulating extra stuff entraps us. We become enslaved to our possessions because we have to move them, store them, and take care of them.

Not only is physical clutter a problem, but spiritual clutter can consume our souls. When this occurs, we allow our minds to be filled with the trash of the world—fear, anxiety, and worry. We need to toss out the trash—forget our fear, appease our anxiety, and walk away from our worry! We must remember that God is willing to help us; all we need to do is ask! "I asked the Lord for help, and he answered me. He saved me from all that I feared" (Psalm 34:4 NCV).

Clutter can overwhelm you,
When you have too much stuff to attend to.
So you need to throw stuff away,
When clutter is in your way.
If you allow spiritual clutter into your heart,
Then the cares of the world will not depart.
When you find that clutter is consuming your day,
Ask for God's help and pray!

CLEAR AWAY THE CONFUSION

"My dear friends, many false prophets have gone out into the world. So do not believe every spirit, but test the spirits to see if they are from God."

-1 John 4:1 (NCV)

*W*hy is there so much confusion about what Scripture teaches? Why do so many people believe false doctrines? It is because many people do not study, read, and spend time in God's Word, and then they can become confused by false teachers. All of the confusion about the teachings in the Bible comes from Satan and his servants. "This does not surprise us. Even Satan changes himself to look like an angel of light. So it does not surprise us if Satan's servants also make themselves look like servants who work for what is right. But in the end they will be punished for what they do" (2 Corinthians 11:14-15 NCV).

Satan has been confusing and perverting the Word of God since the Garden of Eden. Satan twists the Word of God just enough that it sounds like what we read in the Bible, but it is not the same. Satan uses our liberal culture to make people believe that there are many paths to God; however, this is not what Scripture teaches. We know, "Jesus is the only One who can save people. No one else in the world is able to save us" (Acts 4:12 NCV). Confusion about what the Bible says can give people a false hope of salvation.

Some false teachers do not believe in the deity of Christ. Any doctrine that denies the deity of Christ, the virgin birth, Christ's sinless nature, His actual death, or His physical resurrection is false doctrine. "But if someone claims to be a prophet and does not acknowledge the truth about Jesus, that person is not from God. Such a person has the spirit of the Antichrist, which you heard is coming into the world and indeed is already here" (1 John 4:3 NLT).

Throughout history, our world has been full of false teachers, who are like wolves in sheep's clothing. "Watch out for false prophets. They come to you in sheep's clothing, but inwardly they are ferocious wolves" (Matthew 7:15 NIV). Sometimes, false teachers begin teaching the truth, and then they become involved in scandals.

Many of us are familiar with the Jim Bakker scandal. In the mid-1980s, Jim and his wife, Tammy Faye, hosted *The Jim and Tammy Show*, which became the highest-rated religious program in the United States at that time. Jim and Tammy Faye built a $125 million empire, including a religious theme park in South Carolina. As Jim and Tammy Faye acquired more possessions and power, their followers became increasingly critical of their lavish lifestyle. Their quest for money and power was their downfall, and in 1988, Jim Bakker was indicted on 24 counts of fraud after stealing $158 million from his followers. He was sentenced to 45 years in prison, and he was released on parole in 1994.[1] When famous religious leaders fall from grace, it deters people from Christianity. So, we should be aware of false prophets who try to distract us from what God's Word says. Then we can clear away the confusion!

Satan masquerades as an angel of light;
He tries to confuse believers with what is not right.
He persuades false teachers to mislead,
So we must pick up our Bibles and read.
If we listen to what our liberal culture has to say,
We will be misled and not follow God's way.
Remember that false prophets may lead us into confusion,
So we must know what is real and not an illusion!

Close the Door on the Comparison Trap

"For we dare not count or compare ourselves with those who commend themselves. They who measure themselves by one another and compare themselves with one another are not wise."

-2 Corinthians 10:12 (MEV)

We are constantly bombarded with the highlights and achievements of other people on social media. Because of this, people who spend hours a day on social media sometimes experience lower self-esteem, depression, and anxiety. This is definitely a problem for teenagers and young adults, but all of us can feel the negative effects of constantly comparing ourselves with other people who seem to have everything going great in their lives. We must remember that no one has "perfect" hair, makeup, and clothing all of the time!

We may falsely believe that other people's lives are always better than our lives, but this simply is not true. This thinking comes from the enemy, who wants us to get caught in the comparison trap. It is a trap because it causes us to forget what God has given us and instead focus on what other people have. Satan wants to steal our identity and our joy and make us forget how unique and special we are. He tries to delude, deceive, and destroy us by attempting to persuade us that other people are always better than we are, more important, better looking, and more successful. We must remember that Satan is trying to pull us down into his trap, just as he has always done. In Old Testament times, Cain killed his brother Abel because God was more pleased with Abel's offerings. Joseph's brothers compared their father's love for Joseph with their father's love for them, which caused them to sell Joseph as a slave. King Saul compared how many enemies he had killed in battle with how many David had killed, which led him into an insane desire to kill David.

Satan uses whatever devices he can to make us compare ourselves with others because he knows that we will forget that we are "fearfully and wonderfully made." We must remember that God, in His infinite wisdom, created each one of us as unique individuals, and He loves us just as we are. The apostle Paul reminds us to focus on becoming the best version of ourselves; therefore, we do not need to compare ourselves with others. "Pay careful attention to your own work, for then you get the satisfaction of a job well done, and you won't need to compare yourself to anyone else" (Galatians 6:4 NLT).

If we constantly compare ourselves with the world's standards, which often focus on material possessions, outward appearances, and numbers of social media followers, then we may forget how wonderful our lives truly are. When we start believing that our self-worth is dependent upon what other people think about us, then we need to turn to Jesus. He believed that we were worth dying for! When we look in a mirror and are not happy with the image we see, we must remember that we were created in the magnificent and marvelous image of God. When we feel that we are falling into the comparison trap, we must remember who is pushing us into it—Satan!

The comparison trap fills us with despair,
And the enemy sets this trap everywhere.
If you forget how wonderful you are,
You will fall through this trap really far.
The enemy's trap tries to deceive,
And make you forget what God wants you to believe.
So remember that you are God's priceless treasure,
And He has blessed your life beyond measure!

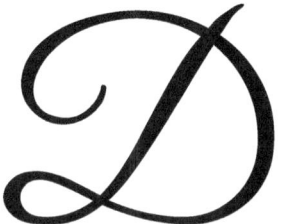

DECREASE YOUR DEBT

*"Let no debt remain
outstanding, except the
continuing debt to love
one another, for whoever
loves others has fulfilled
the law."*

-Romans 13:8 (NIV)

*D*ebt can easily enslave us if we are not careful. Even the very wealthy can go on lavish spending sprees and end up in all-consuming debt. According to a Bloomberg report, 34 million Americans are spending beyond their means, and some people waste their money on unnecessary luxury items. It is so easy to go into debt with a simple swipe of a credit card. With the average credit card interest at 24%, if you had a balance of $5,000 and made only the minimum payment each month, you would end up spending $23,000 for a $5,000 bill! Some people cannot seem to break the cycle of credit card debt, either from a lack of financial knowledge or the desire to appear to be wealthier than they actually are.

According to a Wells Fargo survey, 34% of affluent millennials (people born between the early 1980s and the late 1990s) lie about their income in order to appear financially successful. These people buy designer clothing, purchase expensive sports cars, and travel to exotic destinations just to impress their friends. Almost half of these affluent millennials have gone into debt, spending money extravagantly in order to fake being rich. "Some people pretend to be rich but really have nothing. Others pretend to be poor but really are wealthy" (Proverbs 13:7 NCV). Why are people willing to become slaves to things of no lasting value? Rather than being a slave to money, we should be a servant of God. "No one can serve two masters. For you will hate one and love the other; you will be devoted to one and despise the other. You cannot serve God and be enslaved to money" (Matthew 6:24 NLT).

We should not let debt weigh us down either financially or emotionally. According to *Forbes*, debt affects our mental health, and over half of Americans with debt often suffer from anxiety, sleeplessness, and depression. To compound these problems, stress from debt often causes people to incur more debt.

The best ways to prevent excessive debt are very simple.

- Live within your means.
- Do not make foolish purchases.
- Pay your bills on time.

We must remember that our money and possessions belong to God—we are only stewards, not owners. As good stewards, our only debt is the continuing debt to love others, which Jesus commands us to do. Because Jesus paid the debt for our sins when He died on the cross, we should be forever grateful to Him, and we should faithfully show our gratitude for His payment of our debt by loving Him and loving others.

If you let debt control your life, then you will be filled with strife. If you allow money to control you, then you may feel sad and blue. Remember, the best debt you should owe is a debt of gratitude to Jesus for saving your soul!

If we allow money to become our master,
We will go into debt faster.
And a life filled with excessive debt
Is a life we will regret.
If we are in the habit of paying bills on time,
We will be filled with peace sublime.
The only debt we should have is love,
Which is sent to us from heaven above.

DEPART FROM DESPAIR

"We are hard pressed on every side, but not crushed; perplexed, but not in despair."

-2 Corinthians 4:8 (NIV)

*D*espair is the complete loss of hope, and it can weigh us down when we succumb to it. Circumstances can press in around us to the point that we cannot see a way out.

One person who could have succumbed to despair but did not is former U.S. Navy Commander Porter Halyburton. On October 17, 1965, Halyburton and VF-84 pilot Lieutenant Commander Stan Olmstead were shot down over North Vietnam. Olmstead died in the crash, and Halyburton became a prisoner of war at Hoa Lo Prison, also known as the Hanoi Hilton. Halyburton was held captive for almost seven and a half years, and he suffered brutal punishment while he was a POW. When he was finally released from the Hanoi Hilton, he decided to forgive his captors rather than allow hatred for them to corrode his soul. Halyburton stated that he made it through his agonizing experience by never giving up and falling into despair.[1]

Another man who became a prisoner of war was Lloyd Ponder, who fought on the Bataan peninsula in the Philippines during World War II. Bataan fell to Japan on April 9, 1942, and American and Filipino troops were rounded up and marched to POW camps in the Bataan Death March. During this excruciating 65-mile march through the sweltering jungles of the Philippines, approximately 10,000 men died. Ponder escaped the march; however, he became a POW, and he suffered the brutality of various POW camps for three and a half years. Finally, on August 15, 1945, Japan agreed to an unconditional surrender, and the POW camps were liberated. After his release, Ponder stated that he survived the horrendous conditions of the POW camps because of daily prayer and a firm belief that God would sustain him no matter how hopeless his circumstances were.[2]

Porter Halyburton and Lloyd Ponder both faced terrible situations, but they did not succumb to despair because of their strong faith that God was with them. Most of us will never face the agonizing conditions of a POW camp; however, we will suffer loss of loved ones, sickness, job loss, or natural disasters. When we are completely beaten down, we may be tempted to give up and turn away from God. However, the apostle Paul reminds us in 2 Corinthians 4:16-18 (NIV), "Therefore, we do not lose heart. Though outwardly we are wasting away, yet inwardly we are being renewed day by day. For our light and momentary troubles are achieving for us an eternal glory that far outweighs them all. So we fix our eyes not on what is seen, but on what is unseen, since what is seen is temporary, but what is unseen is eternal."

The apostle Paul suffered many hardships, yet he did not despair because his hope was not based on earthly circumstances. He knew that whether he lived or died, whether he had plenty or nothing, God was in control. We must remember that God will impart hope in us, so we can depart from despair!

If we give in to despair,
We do not see God's hope everywhere.
If we feel our hope slipping away,
We should lean on God and always pray.
We must remember when we experience pain,
It is temporary and will not remain.
We should turn to God and not lose heart
Because His love guides us and will not depart.

DITCH YOUR DOUBTS

"Immediately Jesus reached out his hand and caught him. 'You of little faith,' he said, 'why did you doubt?'"

-Matthew 14:31 (NIV)

We are all familiar with the story of Jesus walking on the water and Peter stepping out of his boat to walk toward Jesus. When Peter steps out of his boat, his faith is strong because his eyes are focused on Jesus, but when Peter takes his eyes off of Jesus and focuses on the storm around him, he begins sinking in the water. We will face storms in our lives, and the only way to survive these storms is to keep our focus on the only one who can lead us through the storms.

Satan wants us to take our eyes off Jesus and focus on the chaos around us, because then we will begin to doubt the goodness of God. It may become easy to doubt God's goodness when we experience the death of a child, an incurable cancer, or an act of violence. Satan tries to convince us that if God were truly good, then these horrible things would not happen. But we must remember God's promises of deliverance from pain and suffering, and the only way we know these promises is to read God's Word, which is one of the weapons Satan fears.

Without the foundation of God's Word, it is easy to fall prey to the poisonous darts that Satan aims at us daily. One of Satan's tactics is to try to convince us that we do not have time to read God's Word; however, we all have time for what we deem important in our lives! When we neglect spending time with God in His Word, then we begin believing what the world says rather than what God tells us is true. Also, when we neglect spending time in prayer, then it becomes easier to allow doubt to get a foothold in our lives. Talking and listening to the Creator of the universe should be a priority in our lives. We should not allow the distractions of everyday life to keep us from communicating with God. James 1:6 (NIV) reminds us, "But when you ask, you must believe and not doubt, because the one who doubts is like a wave of the sea, blown and tossed by the wind."

Because we are human, we have doubts in our lives, and oftentimes these doubts lead us on a spiritual journey of asking questions and seeking understanding. After Jesus' resurrection, the disciple Thomas doubted that Jesus had really risen from the grave. Thomas said, "Unless I see in his hands the mark of the nails, and place my hand into his side, I will never believe" (John 20:25 ESV). Then Jesus appeared to Thomas and invited him to do what he requested. After Thomas saw the scars on Jesus, Thomas believed! Thomas' transformation teaches us that experiencing doubt can strengthen our faith.

Another disciple who had doubts was Peter. After Peter had denied Jesus three times, he experienced doubt and fear. However, Peter's doubts dissipated when the resurrected Jesus restored Peter's faith and empowered him to be the foundation of the church. When we keep our eyes upon the foundation of our faith, then our doubts will not destroy us! We must ditch our doubts and throw them out!

We should not allow doubt to destroy our life.
If we do, our days will be filled with strife.
The enemy injects doubt with his poisonous darts,
Which he aims at our souls and our hearts.
He makes us question our faith in order to deceive,
And he makes us wonder why we believe.
So, in order to deter doubt from destroying us,
We need to read God's Word and follow Jesus.

E

ELIMINATE EXCUSES

"But they all alike began to make excuses. The first said, 'I have just bought a field, and I must go and see it. Please excuse me.'"

-Luke 14:18 (NIV)

*E*xcuses! Excuses! We have all heard them, and we have all made them! I heard many ridiculous excuses from my students when I was a college professor. Some memorable ones were:

- "I was waiting for my cat to have kittens, so I could not get my paper done."
- "I had to wash my hair, so I didn't have time to buy ink for my printer."
- "I could not make it to class on time because my phone alarm did not work."

When listening to these excuses, it was obvious that these students were not interested in successfully completing their writing assignments, and they were casting the blame on other situations instead of taking responsibility for their own actions.

- Do not blame others for your mistakes. Blaming others for our mistakes is nothing new. In the third chapter of Genesis, Adam blames Eve for giving him the apple to eat, and he also indirectly blames God for creating Eve. Then Eve blames the serpent for deceiving her. When we make excuses for our mistakes, we will never move on in our lives. Everyone sins, but God is willing to forgive us, so we have no excuse for staying in our past mistakes.

- Do not keep sinning. Excuses to stay in the stranglehold of sin are prevalent. "Everybody is doing it," "Nobody's perfect," "I didn't know it was wrong," "God was tempting me." It is so easy to deceive ourselves with our excuses to keep sinning, but excuses can add up like a pile of dirty laundry. If we keep adding to the pile and never wash the laundry, we will run out of clean clothes! If we allow a lifetime of excuses to pile up, we will run out of time to truly repent of our sins.

- Do not pass up your invitation. In the parable of the Great Banquet, many people turned down their invitation to dine with the king because the timing was inconvenient. We can resist or delay responding to God's invitation with excuses of work duties, family responsibilities, or financial obligations; however, God's invitation to spend eternity with Him is the most important event in our lives. Jesus reminds us that the time will come when God will rescind His invitation and offer it to others—then it will be too late for all of our lame excuses! "I tell you, not one of those who were invited will get a taste of my banquet" (Luke 14:24 NIV).

We should not allow excuses to get in our way; we must respond to God's invitation without delay!

If we make excuses for everything we do,
We will fail to see what is true.
If we say we don't have time for Jesus,
One of these days, He will not invite us.
We will not spend eternity with Him,
Because His invitation He will rescind.
We should not let our excuses cause us to be late
To dine with the King and to have a life that is great!

ESCAPE FROM ENVY

"A heart at peace gives life to the body, but envy rots the bones."

-Proverbs 14:30 (NIV)

$\mathcal{E}$nvy is defined as "a resentful, dissatisfied longing for another's possessions, position, fortune, achievements, or success." Envy is a poisonous root that will fester and grow until it consumes its victim.

The effects of envy are evident in the William Shakespeare play *Othello*. In this classic play, the protagonist is Othello, a general in the Venetian army, and the antagonist is the evil Iago, an officer. Envy begins to fester in Iago's heart when Othello promotes Cassio to the position of lieutenant instead of Iago, so Iago decides to take revenge on Othello. Iago devises a plot to make Othello believe that his wife, Desdemona, is having an affair with Cassio. Iago does this by placing Desdemona's handkerchief in Cassio's room. Then Iago tells Othello, "Oh, beware, my lord, of jealousy! It is the green-eyed monster which doth mock the meat it feeds on" (Act 3, Scene 3). Iago knows that this statement will spur Othello to become jealous of Cassio.

Iago hates both Othello and Cassio, and he wants both of them dead. Iago's deviousness leads him to get Roderigo, who is in love with Desdemona, to kill Cassio. Iago steals jewels, and he tells Roderigo that he will give the jewels to Desdemona in order to persuade her to fall in love with Roderigo. When Roderigo fails to kill Cassio, Iago kills Roderigo, so he will not have to confess to

45

stealing the jewels. In the meantime, Othello found Desdemona's handkerchief in Cassio's room and became enraged, so he killed his ever-faithful wife, Desdemona. After he kills her, Emilia, Iago's wife, tells Othello that Desdemona was faithful to him. Then Iago kills Emilia, and Othello kills himself. Iago's envy caused the deaths of four people. "For where you have envy and selfish ambition, there you find disorder and every evil practice" (James 3:16 NIV).

Envy is a powerful emotion that can destroy us. It can cause destructive behavior and can lead to murder, rebellion, and rejection of God's truth. The Pharisees' envy of Jesus is a recurring theme in the Gospels. The Pharisees were the elite religious leaders of their time, and they became envious of Jesus' popularity, considering Him a threat to their authority. Jesus knew that the Pharisees were envious of Him. "For he knew that they had handed him over out of envy" (Matthew 27:18 MEV). The Pharisees were more concerned with their own status rather than the truth in God's Word. Their envy blinded them to the truth.

Envy fuels a fire of destruction in our lives, and it burns everything in its path. We will never be happy if we continue to fuel the fire of envy in our hearts. Envy corrodes our hearts with its poisonous darts, so the best thing we can do is to escape from envy before it captures us in its deadly desires!

We must escape from the clutches of envy;
It blinds people to truth, so they cannot see.
Envy is a green-eyed monster filled with pains,
That plagues its victims with grief that remains.
Envy will eat away at your heart and soul,
And once it does, you are not whole.
It is best to prevent envy from entering your heart,
Because once it does, it is slow to depart.

EXERCISE EVERY DAY

"Dear friend, I hope all is well with you and that you are as healthy in body as you are strong in spirit."

-3 John 1:2 (NLT)

$\mathcal{G}$od is concerned for both your body and your soul. As a responsible Christian, you should neither neglect nor indulge yourself but care for your physical needs and discipline your body so that you are at your best for God's service.

I know that it is challenging to exercise every day, and I do not always adhere to my own advice; however, when I am moving rather than motionless, I feel better physically, emotionally, and spiritually! All of us should find physical activities we enjoy so that exercising is fun, rather than something to check off our to-do lists! I love to walk, dance, and work in my five-acre yard. Now that I am retired, my days consist of less sitting and more moving! I babysit for my very active grandchildren, clean my house and my parents' house, and do volunteer work. I try to adhere to this statement: "She is energetic and strong, a hard worker" (Proverbs 31:17 NLT).

We should honor God with our bodies because we are created in God's image, and our bodies ultimately belong to God. Therefore, we should strive to maintain physical fitness by exercising. According to the Mayo Clinic, there are many benefits of exercise:

1. Consistent exercise can help prevent excess weight gain and help control your weight.
2. Exercise helps prevent or manage many health problems, including stroke, high blood pressure, Type 2 diabetes, depression, anxiety, many types of cancer, arthritis, and falls.
3. Exercise improves mood because physical activity stimulates many brain chemicals that make us feel happier, more relaxed, and less anxious.
4. Exercise boosts energy. Regular physical activity can improve your muscle strength and boost your endurance.
5. Exercise promotes better sleep.

A challenge in our society today is the increase in sedentary lifestyles. Technology has improved our lives in many ways; however, it contributes to our lack of activity. According to the World Health Organization (WHO), sedentary lifestyles increase all causes of mortality, double the risk of cardiovascular disease, diabetes, and obesity, and increase the risks of colon cancer, high blood pressure, osteoporosis, depression, and anxiety. Also, according to the WHO, 60 to 85% of people in the world lead sedentary lifestyles, and it is estimated that nearly two-thirds of children are insufficiently active, which increases their risks of lifelong health problems.

God has given each one of us a body to use and enjoy. It will not last forever, but we should all take care of our bodies, which are designed by God for physical activity. Muscles, bones, and organs deteriorate when we are not active. The self-control required to achieve physical fitness can help us establish better spiritual habits. Persevering during physical challenges can help us learn to persevere while enduring spiritual difficulties. The self-control required to resist unhealthy food or the temptation to be lazy can help us become more effective in resisting sin. "Training your body helps you in some ways, but serving God helps you in every way by bringing you blessings in this life and in the future life, too" (1 Timothy 4:8 NCV).

When we exercise every day,
We may keep health problems at bay.
When we get up and walk and run,
We will always have more fun.
Exercise makes us physically fit,
And we must be disciplined and commit.
Remember that God is concerned with our body and soul,
Because He created us a perfect whole.

FLEE FROM FEAR

"Have I not commanded
you? Be strong and
courageous. Do not
be afraid; do not be
discouraged, for the Lord
your God will be with you
wherever you go."

-Joshua 1:9 (NIV)

Imagine the fear that Christian martyrs throughout history have faced! What sustained these martyrs was the reality that God was with them through everything they endured.

Perpetua (AD 182-203) was a young mother and daughter of a prosperous family living in Carthage in the 2nd century. She became a part of the Christian community even though her father tried to convince her to renounce her Christian faith. Sometime after AD 201, the Roman emperor Septimius Severus forbade conversion to Christianity. Perpetua and four other Christians were arrested. They were tried, and they refused to renounce their beliefs; therefore, they were condemned to death in the arena. Perpetua began a diary while she was imprisoned, and on the night before her scheduled execution, she gave her diary to another Christian, who described Perpetua's bravery in the arena when she was attacked by wild beasts. She survived the attacks, and then she voluntarily accepted her death by the sword. She was only 22 years old.[1]

Another Christian martyr was Saint Thomas Becket (1118-1170), who served as Archbishop of Canterbury from 1162 to 1170. Before his appointment as Archbishop, he was the chancellor of England under King Henry II. Becket was one of King Henry's closest confidantes, and he was known for his diplomatic skills, which he used to strengthen royal power. When King Henry II appointed Becket as Archbishop, he hoped to reinforce royal control over the church; however, Becket believed this was unethical, and he stuck to his Christian beliefs. King Henry II was angered by Becket's beliefs, so he ordered the murder of Becket. He was killed in Canterbury Cathedral by four knights who were loyal to King Henry.[2]

Both of these martyrs definitely had to combat fear! Fear is such a powerful emotion that it can incapacitate us and inhibit our abilities. God does not want us to live in fear—but Satan does. We are in a constant spiritual battle, and the enemy wants us to be afraid. But God tells us, "Don't be afraid, for I am with you. Don't be discouraged, for I am your God. I will strengthen you and help you. I will hold you up with my victorious right hand" (Isaiah 41:10 NLT). God is always with us, but this does not mean that nothing bad will ever happen to us. The key to overcoming fear is total and complete trust in God.

We must choose to flee from fear and follow our faith even when things do not make sense in our lives. Remember when God told Gideon to use an army of 300 men to fight the Midianite army of 135,000 men? This did not make sense to Gideon; however, he listened to what God told him. Gideon and his small army surrounded the Midianite camp at night, and, at a signal, smashed jars, blew trumpets, and yelled. Torches were in the jars, and the Midianite army became so confused that they began to fight and kill each other. The Midianites were fearful of what they thought was a huge army. But Gideon's army was not filled with fear because they relied on God. Sometimes when we are faced with fear, the best thing to do is flee from it!

Fear is not our master,
Even when we face disaster.
Fear is not in control
Because God cares for our soul.
We must remember that we have nothing to fear
When we trust in God to always be near.
God promises to be with us whatever we face,
And His strength will uplift us in every place.

Follow the Good Shepherd

*"I am the good shepherd;
I know my sheep and my
sheep know me."*

-John 10:14 (NIV)

I had never been around sheep
until my granddaughters got sheep to show at their county 4-H
fair. Raising sheep is a lot of work, from mucking their stalls to
shearing them in the summer. But it is also fun! My granddaughters witnessed the birth of a lamb, and they were able to hold the
precious little lamb after its birth. My granddaughters learned that
sheep are completely dependent on their shepherd for provision and
protection. Sheep are very slow animals that cannot escape pred-
ators; they have no camouflage and no weapons of defense, such
as claws, sharp hooves, or powerful jaws. Sheep need protection
from harm just as we do.

We have a good shepherd who wants to protect us from harm.
"The Lord is my shepherd; I shall not want. He makes me lie down
in green pastures; He leads me beside still waters. He restores my
soul; He leads me in paths of righteousness for his name's sake"
(Psalm 23:1-3 MEV). David, the author of the 23rd Psalm, was a
shepherd before he was a king, and he compared his relationship
with God to that of a shepherd and his sheep. When sheep are left
to fend for themselves, they are vulnerable and helpless animals,
incapable of providing for their own needs. When sheep go astray,
they are in danger of getting lost, being attacked, or falling off cliffs.

Thankfully, our Good Shepherd protects us from harm. He leads us to the green pastures and the still waters. When we follow anyone or anything other than our Good Shepherd, we get lost and weighed down by the burdens of life. We start blindly following every new trend that promises to make our lives better. When we follow the Good Shepherd, He restores our souls. "Even though I walk through the valley of the shadow of death, I will fear no evil; for You are with me; Your rod and Your staff, they comfort me" (Psalm 23:4 MEV). Death casts a frightening shadow because we are completely helpless in its presence. Only one person can walk with us through death's dark valley—the Good Shepherd. God provides all we need, like a loving shepherd caring for his flock.

The Good Shepherd gave His life on the cross for us. "I am the good shepherd. The good shepherd lays down his life for the sheep. The hired hand is not the shepherd and does not own the sheep. So when he sees the wolf coming, he abandons the sheep and runs away. Then the wolf attacks the flock and scatters it" (John 10:11-12 NIV). A hired hand tends the sheep for money, while the shepherd owns the sheep and is committed to them. Our Good Shepherd knows us by name, and He always leads us in the right direction. We were once lost sheep, but now we have been found. "For you were like sheep going astray, but now you have returned to the Shepherd and Overseer of your souls" (1 Peter 2:25 NIV).

Our Good Shepherd will protect us and provide for us; He will keep us safe and secure; He will be with us wherever we go and whatever we face.

We are like sheep who can easily get lost,
But our Good Shepherd will find us no matter the cost.
Our Good Shepherd will lead us in the right direction,
And He will be with us when we need correction.
Our Good Shepherd will protect us from harm,
So we do not need to be filled with alarm.
He will protect us and restore our soul;
He will always be with us and make us whole.

FORGIVE OTHERS

*"Bear with each other
and forgive one another
if any of you has a
grievance against
someone. Forgive as the
Lord forgave you."*

-Colossians 3:13 (NIV).

*E*ric Lomax, a British soldier, was constantly tortured when he was a prisoner of war during World War II. When British soldiers surrendered to the Japanese in Singapore in 1942, some of the soldiers were sent to Thailand and forced to build the Burma Railway, also known as the Death Railway. More than 12,000 Allied prisoners of war and tens of thousands of forced laborers died building this railway. Eric Lomax was repeatedly beaten by one man, Nagase Takashi, who was an interpreter. After World War II was over, Lomax wanted to find Nagase Takashi so he could kill him; however, when Lomax finally met him, he changed his mind when Takashi cried out that he was truly sorry for the cruel punishment that he had inflicted upon Lomax. Because of Takashi's humility and sorrow, Lomax forgave him.[1]

Forgiveness is a decision of the will. Since God commands us to forgive, we must make a choice to obey God and forgive. The offender may not deserve forgiveness and may not ever change, but we must still forgive. It is impossible to truly forget sins that have been committed against us; however, as much as possible, we should forget what is behind and strive toward what is ahead. Also, forgiving someone does not mean that we are downplaying a wrongdoing or seeking reconciliation with the offender. Furthermore, forgiving someone does not mean that we will ever trust that person again.

The most well-known teaching on unforgiveness is Jesus' parable of the unmerciful servant. In the parable, a king forgives an enormous debt of one of his servants. Later, however, that same servant refuses to forgive the small debt of another man. The king hears about this and rescinds his prior forgiveness. We are to forgive as God has forgiven us. "Be kind and loving to each other, and forgive each other just as God forgave you in Christ" (Ephesians 4:32 NCV). We are completely unworthy, yet Jesus chose to pay the price for our sins and to grant us forgiveness. When we truly grasp the greatness of God's gift to us, we will pass the gift along to others.

Unforgiveness robs us of the full life God intends for us. Rather than promoting justice, our unforgiveness festers into bitterness. "Work at living in peace with everyone, and work at living a holy life, for those who are not holy will not see the Lord. Look after each other so that none of you fails to receive the grace of God. Watch out that no poisonous root of bitterness grows up to trouble you, corrupting many" (Hebrews 12:14-15 NLT).

Unforgiveness eats away at our souls, and it harms us more than the person who wronged us. According to a Johns Hopkins study, unforgiveness is linked to higher incidences of stress, heart disease, high blood pressure, lowered immune response, anxiety, depression, and other health issues. Unforgiveness harms both our souls and our bodies, so it is best to find a way to forgive!

Unforgiveness can eat away at our soul;
It leaves us feeling empty—not whole.
Unforgiveness makes us feel stressed,
And it also causes us to be depressed.
We must remember that God forgave us
When He sacrificed His Son, Jesus.
So if we want to truly live,
We must fully forgive!

G

GET RID OF YOUR GUILT

"So now, those who are in Christ Jesus are not judged guilty."

-Romans 8:1 (NCV)

*I*n the poem, "The Rime of the Ancient Mariner," by Samuel Taylor Coleridge, the ancient mariner shoots an albatross (a large bird), which had been following his ship. After he does this, the ship encounters many problems. The other sailors believe that killing the albatross caused the problems, so they force the ancient mariner to hang the dead bird around his neck. It seems absurd that the ancient mariner would wear a dead bird on his neck just because the other sailors told him to do so. Isn't it absurd that we carry our past sins with us just because Satan tries to convince us that our sins are not forgiven? The ancient mariner should have thrown the albatross into the sea, just as God throws our sins into the sea! "You will have mercy on us again; you will conquer our sins. You will throw away all our sins into the deepest part of the sea" (Micah 7:19 NCV).

Many people struggle with false guilt. They are forgiven, yet they still feel guilty. They may believe that God has forgiven them, but they cannot forgive themselves. Satan wants to paralyze us in our guilt and trap us in the anxiety and depression caused by guilt. He tries to convince us that we must continue to carry our load of guilt because we deserve it. True feelings of guilt lead us to God, whereas false feelings of guilt lead us away from God, which is where Satan wants us to be. We start believing that every time we make a mistake, we are a failure, and we can never be forgiven. However, God paid a high price so we could be free of guilt. We are not designed to carry the weight of our guilt—Jesus did that for us. "He canceled the debt, which listed all the rules we failed to follow. He took away that record with its rules and nailed it to the cross" (Colossians 2:14 NCV). Because of Christ's sacrifice for us, we no longer need to suffer under the burden of guilt.

In Christ, even the most heinous sins are blotted out. Salvation is by grace, and grace forgives. After a person is saved, he will still sin; when he does, God still promises forgiveness. However, Satan tries to make us believe that our sins are so bad that we can never be forgiven. Satan tries to drive a wedge between us and God. But Psalm 103:12 tells us that when God forgives, He truly forgives. "As far as the east is from the west, so far has he removed our transgressions from us" (Psalm 103:12 NIV).

The phrase "as far as the east is from the west" is meant to communicate infinite space. East is one direction, and west is the other. This is different from north and south—you can travel north only so far (to the geographic north pole) before being forced to travel south; therefore, north and south meet at the poles. But east and west never meet; no matter how far you travel east, you will never reach a point at which your next step must be westward. Therefore, our sins have been removed from us as far as it is possible to imagine.

Remember that God's grace gets rid of our guilt, and Satan's condemnation causes us to carry our guilt. Because Christ carried our sins to the cross, we do not need to be burdened by our guilt anymore! We need to get rid of our guilt!

The grace of God pardons us from our sin,
So we should not allow guilt to win.
Past guilt should not trouble our soul,
Because the forgiveness of Jesus has made us whole.
We should not carry our guilt with us,
Because it was nailed to the cross with Jesus.
Christ's death on the cross declared us "not guilty"
So we should get rid of guilt because we are free!

GIVE MORE THAN
YOU TAKE

*"Give, and it will be given
to you. A good measure,
pressed down, shaken
together and running over,
will be poured into your lap.
For with the measure you
use, it will be measured to you."*

-Luke 6:38 (NIV)

Generous people leave legacies that outlive their lives. Praise God for people like Andrew Carnegie (1835-1919), who amassed a fortune in the steel industry and then became a major philanthropist. Carnegie was born in a poor family in Scotland, and his family moved to the U.S. in 1848, seeking a better life. Carnegie had little formal education, and he took a job as a bobbin boy in a cotton factory, making $1.20 per week. He was ambitious and hard-working, and by the time he was in his early 30s, he was a wealthy man. In the early 1870s, he co-founded his first steel company. In 1901, John Pierpont Morgan purchased Carnegie Steel for $480 million, making Andrew Carnegie one of the wealthiest men in the world.

After this, Carnegie devoted himself to philanthropy, and in 1889, he wrote an essay titled "The Gospel of Wealth." In this essay, he stated that the rich have "a moral obligation to distribute their money in ways that promote the welfare and happiness of the common man." He also said, "The man who dies rich dies disgraced." Carnegie eventually gave away $350 million (the equivalent of billions of dollars today). He established more than 2,500 public libraries around the world, donated more than 7,600 organs to churches worldwide, and endowed organizations dedicated to research in science, education, and world peace.[1]

God's Word is clear that the generous are remembered and rewarded, whether in this life or the next. We can be generous with our resources, our time, our hospitality, and our friendship. In our generosity, we are not to expect repayment because our reward will come from the Lord, in His way, in His time. The Lord told the prophet Elijah to find a widow in Zarephath and that she would provide for him. But when Elijah found her, she did not have enough food for herself and her son to survive. Nevertheless, she was generous, and she gave Elijah the only food she had left. Then the Lord filled her jars of flour and oil, ensuring they were never empty. The widow's generosity was rewarded.

The person who gives only a little will receive only a little in return. "Remember this: Whoever sows sparingly will also reap sparingly, and whoever sows generously will also reap generously" (2 Corinthians 9:6 NIV). If you are stingy, you reap sorrow. If you are generous, you reap goodness. The more you give, the more you get in return! You will be blessed beyond measure when you give what you treasure.

The apostle Paul reminds us, "I showed you in all things that you should work as I did and help the weak. I taught you to remember the words Jesus said, 'It is more blessed to give than to receive'" (Acts 20:35 NCV).

Generous people are a blessing to everyone;
They exemplify the teachings of God's Son.
Generous people give away time and treasure,
And they often find they are blessed beyond measure.
Generous people find ways to help the needy,
Rather than always being greedy.
Generous people know it is better to give than to receive,
Because in God's Word, they truly believe.

GUARD AGAINST GOSSIP

"A troublemaker plants seeds of strife; gossip separates the best of friends."

-Proverbs 16:28 (NLT)

An old story tells of a woman who repeated gossip about her neighbor, and soon the whole town knew about it. Later, the woman who spread the rumors learned that they were not true. Because she was sorry for what she had done, she went to an elder in the town who was known for his wisdom. He told her to get a bag of feathers and drop individual feathers along a road. The woman did that, and then she returned to the elder the next day. He told her to go and collect the feathers and bring them back to him. The woman searched for the feathers along the road and could not find them because the wind had carried them away. She returned to the elder, who said, "It's easy to scatter feathers but impossible to get them back." This is true about gossip! It is easy to spread hurtful words, but once you do, you can never completely undo the damage.

Gossip destroys friendships. It drives a wedge between people that might never go away. Gossipers often speak of the faults and failures of other people or reveal potentially embarrassing or shameful details of someone's life. Before we repeat anything about someone else, we should make sure that we have all of the facts. We should also decide if the information we are repeating will do more harm than good. "Mean-spirited slander is heartless; quiet discretion accompanies good sense. A gadabout gossip can't be trusted with a secret, but someone of integrity won't violate a confidence" (Proverbs 11:12-13 MSG).

Gossip destroys lives. Spreading false information can have horrible consequences. According to Pew Research, nearly half of U.S. teens have experienced cyberbullying. Offensive name-calling and spreading false rumors are the most reported types of cyberbullying. Tragically, cyberbullying may lead to depression, anxiety, loneliness, low self-esteem, substance abuse, and suicide. Some people look for opportunities to destroy other people. As Christians, we are commanded to love others; therefore, we should look for ways to build one another up rather than to destroy them by spreading false rumors. "When you talk, do not say harmful things, but say what people need—words that will help others become stronger. Then what you say will do good to those who listen to you" (Ephesians 4:29 NCV).

Gossip destroys our souls. Satan wants us to spread lies and rumors about other people because he is the father of lies. When we delight in bringing other people down, we are really bringing ourselves down. Destroying other people destroys our souls. When we spread false information about other people, we show how false our religion is. "If you claim to be religious, but don't control your tongue, you are fooling yourself, and your religion is worthless" (James 1:26 NLT).

We must guard against gossip each day because it destroys lives and takes friendships away!

Gossip can tear people apart;
It can drive a spear into someone's heart.
When false rumors and hurtful words are repeated,
They can never be truly deleted.
When we repeat things that are not true,
We cause others to feel sad and blue.
So we must stop spreading words of hate,
Because once a life is destroyed, it is too late!

HAND OVER THE REMOTE CONTROL

"Then Jesus went to work on his disciples. 'Anyone who intends to come with me has to let me lead. You're not in the driver's seat; I am.'"

-Matthew 16:24 (MSG)

*A*t our house, I like to be in charge of the remote control when my husband and I are watching television. Call me a control freak if you will! There is something about trying to be in control that draws me in. This simple example makes me realize that I try to control situations over which I have no control, and I know that if I surrender control to God, my life will be better!

Surrender is a battle term. It implies giving up all rights to the conqueror. When an opposing army surrenders, they lay down their weapons. Surrendering to God works in the same way. God has a plan for our lives, and surrendering to Him means that we set aside our own plans and seek His plan for our lives. And along the way, we find that God's plan is always the best! "For I know the plans I have for you, declares the Lord, plans to prosper you and not to harm you, plans to give you hope and a future" (Jeremiah 29:11 NIV). Sometimes our own plans lead to destruction. "There is a way that appears to be right, but in the end it leads to death" (Proverbs 14:12 NIV).

God demands that we surrender all to Him. The hymn "I Surrender All" reminds us what we must do to follow Christ. The writer of the hymn, Judson Van DeVenter, was born in Michigan in 1855. From an early age, he loved art and music. After attending college, he took a job as supervisor of art for public high schools in Pennsylvania. During this time, he was very active in his church, where he sang in the choir and participated in evangelistic rallies. Some of his friends urged him to pursue full-time ministry; however, his passion was art, and he did not want to give it up for ministry. He struggled for five years trying to decide between his art career and pursuing a career in ministry. Finally, he surrendered all of his life to Christ, and he became an evangelist. After that, he wrote the hymn, "I Surrender All," which contains the line, "All to Thee, my blessed Savior, I surrender all."[1]

Surrendering to anyone or anything is challenging because we want to be in control of our lives. We want to control our finances, our health, our homes, and our children. We can become overwhelmed by a tremendous burden when we try to control things that are definitely beyond our control. Surrendering is also difficult because it goes against everything that society teaches us about self-reliance, but what our hearts truly desire is a Savior who knows what is best for us.

When we surrender our lives to Christ, our selfish, self-indulgent, and sinful lives are transformed into lives of grateful service to Christ, and we are new creations. "If anyone belongs to Christ, there is a new creation. The old things have gone; everything is made new" (2 Corinthians 5:17 NCV). When we become new creations in Christ, we are happy to let Him control our lives.

If we try to control our own life,
We will walk a path full of strife.
But if we surrender our lives to Jesus,
He prospers us and blesses us.
When we surrender all,
He guides us so we will not fall.
When we finally decide to follow and not lead,
We will find joy and happiness indeed!

HELP OTHER PEOPLE

"Bear one another's burdens, and so fulfill the law of Christ."

-Galatians 6:2 (MEV)

When the American Civil War began in 1861, Clara Barton left her job as a recording clerk in the U.S. Patent Office, and she made it her mission to bring supplies to Union soldiers. In 1862, she received official permission to transport supplies to battlefields, where she tended to the wounded and became known as the "Angel of the Battlefield." She was officially named head nurse for one of General Benjamin Butler's units in 1864, even though she had no formal training as a nurse. After the war, Barton helped locate missing soldiers and mark thousands of graves. Twenty years after Clara Barton first began helping soldiers on the battlefields, she founded the American Red Cross with the approval of President Chester A. Arthur.[1]

One person can definitely make a difference in transforming the lives of others. Clara Barton had no idea what a legacy she would leave in establishing the American Red Cross. Many of us are familiar with the Red Cross today because of blood drives in our local communities. It is very easy to register for local blood drives, and I encourage everyone to donate blood because every two seconds, someone in the U.S. needs blood, and only 3% of age-eligible people donate blood each year. Donating blood is something that I have done for many years, and it is an easy and rewarding thing to do to help other people.

Another way that I help other people is by volunteering with Samaritan's Purse, which is a nondenominational evangelical Christian organization. The mission statement for Samaritan's Purse states, "Since 1970, Samaritan's Purse has helped meet the needs of people who are victims of war, poverty, natural disasters, disease, and famine with the purpose of sharing God's love through His Son, Jesus Christ. The organization serves the Church worldwide to promote the Gospel of the Lord Jesus Christ."[2] When I volunteered with Samaritan's Purse to help with disaster relief in Sullivan, Indiana, after a tornado destroyed many homes, it was hard work, but it was worth it. After our team finished the cleanup at each site, we presented the homeowners with a Bible and prayed with them. Another volunteer opportunity with Samaritan's Purse is through Operation Christmas Child. Our local church packs shoeboxes for children each year, and many of us have traveled to the packing center in Boone, North Carolina, to check and repack boxes.

When you help other people reduce the burdens that life has imposed upon them, you are also helping yourself. According to Mayo Clinic, volunteering improves physical and mental health, and it leads to lower rates of depression and anxiety. Volunteering also prevents feelings of isolation, increases your confidence, and makes you happy. In addition, when you volunteer, you feel a sense of purpose and learn valuable skills.

All of us can help other people by sharing our time, talents, and treasures with them. Acts of kindness and sharing are pleasing to God. "And don't forget to do good and to share with those in need. These are the sacrifices that please God" (Hebrews 13:16 NLT).

Helping other people is what you should do,
Because God is pleased, and He will bless you.
God wants you to help others
Because in Christ, we are all sisters and brothers.
When helping others is your goal,
You will find it is always good for your soul.
When you donate your time, talents, and treasure,
You will definitely be blessed beyond measure!

HOLD ON A LITTLE LONGER

*"We can rejoice too,
when we run into
problems and trials, for
we know that they help
us develop endurance.
And endurance develops
strength of character, and character strengthens
our confident hope of salvation."*

-Romans 5:3-4 (NLT)

$\mathcal{B}$ecoming a Christian does not make us immune to life's troubles, but the problems that we encounter will strengthen our character, deepen our trust in God, and give us greater confidence in our glorious future. When we face tragedy in our lives, we may wonder how a loving God would allow us to go through horrible things, such as the death of a child, cancer, natural disasters, or acts of terrorism. But we must remember these words of Jesus: "I have said these things to you, that in me you may have peace. In the world you will have tribulation. But take heart; I have overcome the world" (John 16:33 ESV).

Sometimes, our trials may eventually bless the lives of many people. Most of us are familiar with the song "Just as I Am," which was written by Charlotte Elliott. Charlotte was born in England in 1789, and she was the granddaughter of a minister. She grew up as a happy, carefree girl, but by the time she was 30 years old, her health had declined, and she became a bedridden invalid for the rest of her life. Not only did she suffer physically, but her mental health was also affected. In 1822, when Charlotte was 32 years old, she was living with her married brother. A famous evangelist, Dr. Cesar Malan, visited their home, and he spoke with Charlotte about her salvation. He told her that she needed to come to Christ "just as she was." In 1836, Charlotte was at home alone, feeling sad, and she began reflecting on Dr. Malan's words spoken to her years earlier. After that, she wrote her now-famous hymn, "Just as I Am."[1] This song has been sung thousands of times throughout the years, and it eventually became the song used at the conclusion of Billy Graham's crusades. According to Lifeway Research, an estimated 2.2 billion people have heard Billy Graham preach, and an estimated 2.2 million people have responded to the invitation to give their lives to Christ when the song "Just as I Am" was sung.[2]

Every person will experience pain, sickness, and tragedy in life. We simply need to decide if we are going to face life with or without God. Without God, there is no hope. With God, we have hope because we know that all of our pain will be over in the future, and we know that our faith will become stronger because of the trials we face. Trials are God's tools to break our dependence on ourselves and to teach us to depend on Him.

If we just hold on a little longer, we will have an eternal reward. "Blessed is the one who perseveres under trial because, having stood the test, that person will receive the crown of life that the Lord has promised to those who love him" (James 1:12 NIV). The crown of life is not glory and honor here on Earth, but the reward of eternal life—living with God forever!

When our hope is in Heaven, then we can endure the hardships we face on Earth. If we just hold on a little longer, then we will no longer have to face sorrow and sickness, pain and persecution, or tragedy and trials!

When our trials put us to the test,
We eventually will receive peace and rest.
When we face sickness and pain,
We know that these problems will not remain.
When our lives are not going our way,
We know that there will be a brighter day.
If we can just hold on a little longer,
We will find that our faith will become stronger.

IDENTIFY YOUR INVINCIBILITY

"He gives strength to the weary and increases the power of the weak."

-Isaiah 40:29 (NIV)

*I*n 1982, Tony Cavallo was working under his car, a 1964 Chevy Impala. The jacks failed, and the car fell on him. Angela Cavallo, Tony's mother, lifted the car off her son, holding the car's back end up for about five minutes until neighbors came to assist her and put the jacks back under the car. They were able to pull Tony out, and he survived with only minor scrapes and bruises.

In another miraculous story, 15-year-old Austin Smith momentarily held up the back end of a car, which had fallen on his 72-year-old grandfather. His grandfather sustained fractured ribs, but he survived. Austin said that a burst of adrenaline and God helped him pick up the car.

Another superhuman feat was accomplished by teenagers Hannah and Haylee Smith, who lifted part of a tractor off their father, Jeff Smith. He survived with a broken wrist and minor bumps and bruises.[1]

Angela Cavallo, Austin Smith, and Hannah and Haylee Smith all relied upon hysterical strength, which refers to extraordinary displays of human strength, typically in life-threatening situations. According to Guinness World Records, the heaviest deadlift is 1,104 pounds, which was set by Hafpor Julius Björnsson of Iceland in 2020. If the world record holder can only lift 1,104 pounds, how can ordinary people lift more weight? Most of the time, we only use a fraction of our maximum strength. However, when we are in a life-or-death situation, the fight-or-flight response causes our bodies to release hormones, like adrenaline, cortisol, and endorphins. Adrenaline gives you a temporary boost of strength, cortisol gives you extra energy, and endorphins help reduce your perception of pain.[2] When people must perform superhuman feats, it seems that they are invincible.

Most people will not need to lift vehicles off other people, but we all need extra strength to lift the heavy burdens of life off our shoulders. This is when we must rely on God's power, which is beyond our comprehension. "Now to him who is able to do immeasurably more than we ask or imagine, according to his power that is at work within us" (Ephesians 3:20 NIV). Divine power is at work in our lives every day—we just need to rely upon it. Because God is omnipotent, He possesses all power over all things at all times.

We must also remember that our strength is found in Christ. When we rely on Christ's strength every day, we find a never-ending source of energy, and we will have the strength to endure life's problems and pitfalls. Sometimes when facing a challenging situation, we say to ourselves, "I can do all things through Christ because he gives me strength" (Philippians 4:13 NCV).

The world can be a hard place that tries to knock you out, put you down, and trample on your goals, but God's power and strength will not allow you to fall. When you feel that you can no longer bear the weight of your burdens, identify your invincibility in Christ.

When you feel weak and start to fall,
Seek God's power, which is available to all.
God's strength will make you invincible;
When the world tries to defeat you, you will be unbeatable.
God will supply you with His amazing power,
Which will be with you every hour.
Remember, there is no limit to what God can do.
If you ask Him for strength, He will give it to you.

IGNORE IDOLATRY

"Therefore, my dear friends, flee from idolatry."

-1 Corinthians 10:14 (NIV)

*W*hen we hear the word *idols*, we may envision statues or figurines carved out of wood, stone, or gold. However, in biblical usage, an idol is anything that we place ahead of God in our lives. Most people in modern times do not bow before manmade idols; however, we idolize possessions, success, and ourselves.

- Possessions—How much stuff do we really need? Some celebrities own many homes, have private jets, and numerous vehicles. Our society keeps building bigger houses with extra storage space to accommodate all of our possessions, even if we go into exorbitant debt to pay for all of our stuff. According to the Federal Reserve, only 48% of Americans with credit card debt pay their bills each month. Many of these people buy the newest gadget, which soon breaks, just to maintain their social status. When we worship "things," we will never be satisfied.

- Success—Can success be both good and bad? Yes! It is good to work hard and aim for success in everything we do; however, when we become so obsessed with our careers only to make more money in order to satisfy our insatiable desire for more material possessions, then we "idolize" success. If we are working only to show the world how successful we are, we will find that all our trophies, plaques, and awards will be of no value if they have been acquired at the expense of priceless time spent with our loved ones. If we are working simply to have a "fancy" title, we may miss out on the most important titles: Mom, Dad, Grandma, Grandpa, and the most significant one—Child of God!

- Ourselves—The worship of self in our society has caused us to become self-indulgent. In our affluent society, we indulge in whatever we want, whether it is alcohol, drugs, or food. The number one killer of young people in the U.S. today is drugs. Obesity rates in the U.S. have skyrocketed, and childhood diabetes is epidemic. We should adhere to the advice that we cannot get everything we want, and "everything" is not always good for us. The temptation to indulge in ourselves is so powerful that only Jesus can set us free from this desire. In our liberal society, some churches have even accepted the lies of Satan, and they have strayed away from God's Word in order to accommodate an "anything goes" culture.

We definitely need possessions; we should aim for success, and we should take care of ourselves. However, when we place these "idols" on a pedestal above God, then we become enslaved by them. If we love these idols more than God, then we forsake God's love for us. "Those who cling to worthless idols turn away from God's love for them" (Jonah 2:8 NIV). We must ignore idols and turn to God! He is the only one who can fulfill our hearts' desires.

What satisfaction can an idol bring?
What happens when you place it above everything?
If an idol takes first place in your life,
You will be faced with suffering and strife.
If you worship the worthless idols of society,
You will become enslaved by them and never be free.
Idols will not last and will soon depart,
And you will be left with a broken heart.

IMAGINE YOUR AMAZING FUTURE

"And God will wipe away
every tear from their
eyes; there shall be no
more death, nor sorrow,
nor crying. There shall
be no more pain, for the
former things have passed away."

-Revelation 21:4 (NKJV)

*N*o matter what you are going through, it will be better in the future! There will be no more sickness, no more hatred, no more pain, and no more suffering! Eternity with God will be more wonderful than you could ever imagine! At God's appointed time, the risen Lord Jesus will return for His faithful followers; this will be a glorious day for those who believe in Christ.

Good will triumph over evil. Christ will defeat Satan. When we have confidence in our final destination, we can follow Christ with dedication, no matter what we face, because we know that evil will not last forever. We know that Christ has victory over death. Jesus said, "I am the resurrection and the life. The one who believes in me will live, even though they die" (John 11:25 NIV). Whoever believes in Christ has a spiritual life that death cannot conquer.

Christians should not fear death because we know life with Jesus in eternity will be so much better than we can comprehend. "But as it is written in the Scriptures: 'No one has ever seen this, and no one has ever heard about it. No one has ever imagined what God has prepared for those who love him'" (1 Corinthians 2:9 NCV). Whether we will walk on streets of gold does not matter. What does matter is that we will be with Jesus. Heaven is real, and hell is real! There are only two options for our "forever" home—Heaven or hell. The worst part of hell would be total separation from God. Even those people who ignore God this side of eternity still have the opportunity to have God in their lives before they take their last breath. If they do not accept Jesus as their Savior, then they will be cast into hell. Just as it is impossible to imagine the magnificence of Heaven, it is equally impossible to comprehend the horrors of hell.

When we try to imagine the glory of Heaven, it is impossible! It is almost like trying to imagine a beautiful vacation spot. Even if we look at brochures depicting its beauty, we cannot truly comprehend what it is like until we travel there. How do we know what Heaven will be like? Read God's Word! "In my Father's house are many mansions; if it were not so, I would have told you. I go to prepare a place for you" (John 14:2 NKJV).

Many hymn writers have described how amazing Heaven will be, and one of those writers was Sanford Fillmore Bennett (1836-1898). Bennett owned a drug store in Elkhorn, Wisconsin. A local musician, Joseph P. Webster, who suffered from periods of depression, would often stop by Bennett's store. On one visit, when Webster was especially distraught, Bennett asked Webster what was troubling him, and Webster replied, "It's no matter. It will all be right by and by." Bennett was immediately inspired by these words, and he hurriedly scribbled the lyrics to the classic hymn "In the Sweet By and By." He gave the lyrics to Webster, who composed the music, and within thirty minutes, the two of them were singing: "In the sweet by and by, we shall meet on that beautiful shore."[1] We can only imagine how beautiful Heaven will be!

Living in Heaven is hard to comprehend.
It will be joy and peace without end.
Pain and sorrow will not be there;
Goodness and beauty will be everywhere.
The glory of God will shine bright;
Darkness will not exist—only light!
Suffering and death will not overcome us
When we are safe in Heaven with Jesus.

JOIN TOGETHER WITH OTHERS

"For where two or three gather in my name, there am I with them."

-Matthew 18:20 (NIV)

During the pandemic, when many churches were not meeting in person, it became very easy to stay at home in our pajamas and watch a church sermon online, but we were not truly fellowshipping with others. According to Lifeway Research, American congregations are at 85% of their pre-pandemic attendance levels. In our world today, fellowship with other believers is vital to our faith.

- Fellowship provides encouragement. During the bad times in life, we need other people to lift us up. "Let us think of ways to motivate one another to acts of love and good works. And let us not neglect our meeting together, as some people do, but encourage one another, especially now that the day of his return is drawing near" (Hebrews 10:24-25 NLT). When we meet together, we have opportunities to minister to others. One of the ministries I am involved in at our church is a card ministry. Each of us in our group sends cards each week to encourage and uplift other people.
- Fellowship reminds us that we are not alone. When the prophet Elijah felt like he was the only faithful person left to proclaim God's Word, God reminded him that there were

7,000 other people in Israel who were faithful to Him. God told Elijah, "I have seven thousand people left in Israel who have never bowed down before Baal and whose mouths have never kissed his idol" (1 Kings 19:18 NCV). When we meet together with other believers, we know that we are not alone in our faith. Of the 8 billion people in the world, 2.4 billion are Christians, making Christianity the world's largest religion.

- Fellowship helps us grow in our faith. I love my Bible study group because it helps my understanding of God's Word. Even though everyone in our group has different life experiences, what unites us is our belief in Jesus. "All the believers were together and had everything in common" (Acts 2:44 NIV). Because everyone in our Bible study group shares the same beliefs, we can have honest conversations, not superficial discussions about trivial topics.

- Fellowship makes us stronger. "As iron sharpens iron, so one person sharpens another" (Proverbs 27:17 NIV). Just as rubbing two iron blades together makes them sharper and more useful, having fellowship with others gives us the encouragement to become stronger in our beliefs, making us better able to serve God.

Fellowship with others gives us a sense of community and connection; it makes us feel accountable and accepted, and it blesses and benefits us.

When you join together with one another,
You are united in Christ as sister and brother.
When you gather together in Jesus' name,
Your life is transformed and never the same.
When you meet together as one,
You will be blessed by the Son.
When you come together with love for all,
Your faith will become stronger, and you will not fall.

JUDGE AS JESUS DOES

"Do not judge, or you too will be judged. For in the same way you judge others, you will be judged, and with the measure you use, it will be measured to you."

-Matthew 7:1-2 (NIV)

The Bible's command that we not judge others does not mean we cannot show discernment. Jesus wants us to tell right from wrong. Also, the Bible's command that we not judge others does not mean all actions are equally moral or that truth is relative. The Bible clearly teaches that truth is objective, eternal, and inseparable from God's character. Anything that contradicts the truth is a lie. Likewise, to call adultery or murder a sin is to pass judgment—but it is also agreeing with God. When Jesus said not to judge others, He did not mean that no one can identify sin for what it is.

Some people in our society are very quick to say that Christians are intolerant of others or that Christians are being judgmental. God's Word clearly tells everyone what sin is; therefore, everyone should oppose sin. The Bible's command that we not judge others does not mean there should be no way to deal with sin. In saying, "Do not judge," Jesus was not saying, "Anything goes." Our society today has become increasingly liberal in its views of what is right and what is wrong. However, the Bible has not changed—sin is still sin, even when society tries to water it down!

As Christians, our goal is to lead others to Christ, and this does not happen when we judge incorrectly or harshly. Passing judgment on someone else based solely on appearances is wrong. "Stop judging by mere appearances, but instead judge correctly" (John 7:24 NIV). It is foolish to jump to conclusions about another person before knowing all of the facts about that person. Also, Christians should not be hypocritical in judging others.

> Why do you look at the speck of sawdust in your brother's eye and pay no attention to the plank in your own eye? How can you say to your brother, 'Let me take the speck out of your eye,' when all the time there is a plank in your own eye? You hypocrite, first take the plank out of your own eye, and then you will see clearly to remove the speck from your brother's eye. (Matthew 7:3-5 NIV)

Sometimes the traits that bother us in others are often the habits we dislike in ourselves. Judge yourself first, and then lovingly help other people to change their behavior. We should not point out the sins of other people while we ourselves commit the same sins.

We all need to make wise judgment calls every day. Wisdom tells us that speeding results in accidents, jumping off a bridge causes life-threatening injuries, and taking illegal drugs can kill us. Wisdom should also teach us that continuing to live a life of sin will ultimately result in an eternity in hell. Therefore, it is imperative that the Church and Christians worldwide lovingly judge with discernment and judge as Jesus does!

We must make wise judgment calls every day,
So we must judge as Jesus does and pray.
If we are hypocritical in judging someone,
We are not obeying God's Son.
If we judge someone with hate—not love,
Then we are not following God above.
When judging others, wisdom should guide us,
Then we know we are following Jesus.

JUMP FOR JOY

"May the God of hope
fill you with all joy and
peace as you trust in him,
so that you may overflow
with hope by the power
of the Holy Spirit."

-Romans 15:13 (NIV)

Oftentimes, when we think of "jumping for joy," we picture children jumping for joy at birthday parties or on Christmas morning. Exuberance fills their faces as they open their presents. When I see my grandson jump, he is carefree and happy. If I tried to jump as high as he does, I might fall down and break a bone! I know it is much easier for children to jump than for adults; however, some adults have perfected jumping. According to Guinness World Records, Javier Sotomayor is the current men's high jump world record holder with a jump of 8 feet 0.45 inches! He set this record in 1993, and it still stands! One of the greatest NBA players of all time, Michael Jordan, has the highest vertical jump in NBA history at 48 inches with a hangtime of 0.92 seconds! These are amazing feats!

When our hearts are filled with joy, we do not let the burdens of life weigh us down. The joy of the world is hollow, but the joy found in a personal relationship with the Lord is heavenly. True joy cannot be stolen from us, but we may choose to give our joy away. We should not allow the problems of the world to rob us of our joy. When Jesus was talking to His disciples before His crucifixion, He told them, "Therefore you now have sorrow. But I will see you again, and your heart will rejoice, and no one will take your joy from you" (John 16:22 MEV). Jesus knew that His disciples would be heartbroken at His death, but He knew that they would be with Him again. We should always be filled with joy because Jesus is always with us.

The ability to feel and show joy does not come from the favorable circumstances of life; it comes from God. When Paul and Silas were arrested and put in a Philippian jail cell, they chose joy and started praising the Lord loudly. When the prophet Habakkuk was in a horrible situation, he still rejoiced. "Though the fig tree does not bud and there are no grapes on the vines, though the olive crop fails and the fields produce no food, though there are no sheep in the pen and no cattle in the stalls, yet I will rejoice in the Lord, I will be joyful in God my Savior" (Habakkuk 3:17-18 NIV).

God's people are commanded to rejoice. The apostle Paul tells us, "Rejoice in the Lord always. I will say it again: Rejoice!" (Philippians 4:4 NIV). Paul was in prison when he wrote these words to the Philippians. As Christians, we are to be joyful in every circumstance, even when we have hardships and heartaches, even when we endure suffering and sorrow, even when we face calamities and catastrophes. Whatever life throws at us, we know that Christ is with us. Whenever we feel disheartened, we know that our hearts belong to Christ. When we have the "joy, joy, joy, joy down in our hearts," then nothing can take it from us. When we know that our eternity will be spent with God in Heaven, then we should be filled with joy. We should not let the problems of the world bring us down. Instead, we should "jump for joy"!

When we have joy in our heart,
Our happiness will not depart.
When we do not let life get us down,
We smile, rather than frown.
When having joy is our way of life,
We do not succumb to suffering and strife.
When we choose joy instead of sorrow,
We know everything will be better tomorrow!

KEEP AWAY FROM NEGATIVITY

"Do everything without grumbling or arguing."

-Philippians 2:14 (NIV)

*N*egativity was one of the Israelites' gravest sins after God brought them out of Egypt, parted the Red Sea, and destroyed their enemies. As soon as the Israelites were not getting what they wanted, they started complaining. Rather than rejoicing over everything God had done for them, they moaned and groaned! Christians should model a better approach to life. If Christians are filled with negativity, then why would nonbelievers want to believe? We must combat the world's negativity and demonstrate the abundant life that Jesus has given us!

Unfortunately, bad things will happen to good and bad people alike. But what the world needs to see is how Christians respond to tragedies in their lives. We must remember that Jesus came to give us an abundant life filled with positivity rather than negativity. "The thief does not come except to steal, and to kill, and to destroy. I have come that they may have life, and that they may have it more abundantly" (John 10:10 NKJV).

If the harm a negative person is doing to you exceeds the good you are doing for them, it may be time to stay away from them. God calls us to love others; however, He also warns us against spending too much time with negative people. "Do not be misled: Bad company corrupts good character" (1 Corinthians 15:33 NIV).

Literature is filled with negative characters who spread their malignant beliefs to others. One such character is Miss Havisham from Charles Dickens' novel *Great Expectations*. Miss Havisham is a vengeful recluse who was jilted on her wedding day. From that moment on, she is consumed with bitterness and hatred for humanity, especially men. She wears her tattered wedding dress every day; she has stopped the clocks in her house to remind her of the time when her fiancé left her, and she refuses to get rid of her wedding cake. She adopts a daughter, Estella, whom she raises to be cruel and heartless so she can break men's hearts. When the character Pip falls in love with Estella, she rejects him. Later in the novel, Miss Havisham asks Pip to forgive her when she realizes that his heart was broken in the same manner as her own, but the damage had already been done. Negativity is a bitter poison that affects everyone around it.

It is best to stay away from negative people. "Warn a divisive person once, and then warn them a second time. After that, have nothing to do with them" (Titus 3:10 NIV). Negative people will deplete your positive outlook on life; they will tear you apart with their toxic views.

Life is too short to listen to the caustic critics, follow the negative naysayers, or be around the perennial pessimists. Instead, we need to surround ourselves with people who exude healthy happiness! "So I concluded there is nothing better than to be happy and enjoy ourselves as long as we can" (Ecclesiastes 3:12 NLT).

Negative people will bring you down;
They never smile and always frown.
Their negative attitude is toxic,
And their presence is caustic.
Their hearts are full of bitterness and strife,
And they do not enjoy a happy life.
So it is best to avoid their negativity,
And be around people with positivity.

KNOCK DOWN THE COBWEBS

"What they trust in is fragile; what they rely on is a spider's web."

-Job 8:14 (NIV)

*E*ven though cobwebs may look fragile, they are actually quite strong. According to the Massachusetts Institute of Technology, spider webs are stronger than steel on a pound-for-pound basis. Also, spiders are very industrious, and they can build a web in thirty to sixty minutes. If you do not kill the spiders in your house, you will continue to have cobwebs.

If we do not avoid Satan, he will continue trapping us in his webs of deceit. Satan never rests, and he is busy spinning his poisonous webs every day. Some of his webs may appear harmless, just as some spider webs are quite magnificent. Therefore, we need to be vigilant so we do not become trapped in Satan's devious schemes. "Be sober and watchful, because your adversary the devil walks around as a roaring lion, seeking whom he may devour" (1 Peter 5:8 MEV). Satan is like a lion who will attack straggling animals who are alone and not alert. When we feel alone, weak, helpless, or cut off from other believers, we are most vulnerable to Satan's attacks.

Just as spiders will chase their prey in the direction of their webs in order to corner them, Satan will try to corner us and make us feel like we have no way out of our sinful lives. He will tell us that we are too bad to be saved, or that if God truly loved us, He would not allow evil in the world. These lies have been told to so many people that Satan has become a skilled con artist, weaving his webs of deceit each day; however, Satan cannot defeat us. "'So no weapon that is used against you will defeat you. You will show that those who speak against you are wrong. These are the good things my servants receive. Then victory comes from me,' says the Lord" (Isaiah 54:17 NCV).

The antidote to Satan's poisonous lies is the Word of God. When Satan tempted Jesus in the wilderness, Jesus responded with God's Word. Just like you must hire an exterminator to get rid of spiders in your house, you must rely on the power of God to exterminate Satan's power over your life. If you abandon reading God's Word, then it is easier for Satan to build his poisonous webs in your heart, just as it is easy for spiders to take over an abandoned house.

We must remember that Satan is the enemy of God and truth, and he does everything he can to trap people in his poisonous webs. He portrays evil as good, he distorts the truth, and he exploits our weaknesses. Even though Satan's webs are deadly, Jesus gives us the antidote to Satan's poisonous sting: "O death, where is your victory? O death, where is your sting?" (1 Corinthians 15:55 NLT). Even though Satan seemed to be victorious at the cross of Jesus, God turned Satan's apparent victory into defeat when Jesus rose from the dead. Therefore, as Christians, we should no longer fear death because it has been defeated!

When we knock down the cobwebs each day, we keep Satan at bay!

Satan is busy weaving his webs of deceit each day,
So we must avoid his traps and always pray.
Satan's webs may look magnificent,
But they are malignant and maleficent.
Because Satan's lies can easily deceive,
We must read God's Word in order to believe.
If we have the truth of God in our heart,
Then Satan's lies will not tear us apart.

Know When to Say "No"

"For even when we were with you, we gave you this rule: 'The one who is unwilling to work shall not eat.'"

-2 Thessalonians 3:10 (NIV)

$\mathcal{W}$e should not become burdened by the irresponsible actions of other people. God gives us certain standards when it comes to giving our time and money to other people; however, we must establish healthy boundaries in our lives.

- The goal of boundaries is to make sacrifices for people when appropriate, but never in a destructive manner. We should be available to help people in a crisis, but unavailable for indulgent demands. Healthy boundaries are good for helping people. Enabling the sins or irresponsibility of others is not loving; it is self-indulgent. Wise boundaries allow others to reap the consequences of their actions and hopefully learn from these consequences. "As I have observed, those who plow evil and those who sow trouble reap it" (Job 4:8 NIV). We must tell people "no," just as God tells us "no" when He knows what is in our best interest.
- The help we give to other people should not support laziness but rather establish accountability. When our children

108

are young, we give them responsibilities based on their ages. "No discipline seems pleasant at the time, but painful. Later on, however, it produces a harvest of righteousness and peace for those who have been trained by it" (Hebrews 12:11 NIV). Because we love our children, we want to teach them to have a strong work ethic and not expect society to give them everything they want without working for it. If our society does not teach people how to work and take responsibility for their own actions, then these people will never mature. The old saying, "Give a man a fish and he eats for a day, teach him to fish and he eats for a lifetime," is definitely true.

- When we truly love people, we tell them "no" more than "yes." Giving people help that encourages laziness does not help them. It simply makes these people dependent upon on others for help. We must teach people to take responsibility. As Galatians 6:5 (NCV) says, "Each person must be responsible for himself." When people continue to live irresponsible lives with no accountability for their actions, then we should not encourage their behavior. If we continue to bail people out financially, they will never learn good spending habits.

Telling people "no" may not be easy, but it is necessary if we want to cultivate productive members in our society. When we allow people to live irresponsible lives, they not only harm themselves but also other people as well. Remember that our heavenly Father loves us, cares for us, and protects us, but He also reprimands us when necessary. So, we must know when to say "no."

We need to learn to say "no";
It may be the best way to help others to grow.
If we do not teach people to be accountable,
Their problems may become insurmountable.
If we are always giving a free handout,
People do not learn what life is all about.
If we allow people to be dependent upon society,
Then they never learn to be truly free.

LET GO OF LAZINESS

"The lazy will not get
what they want, but
those who work hard
will."

-Proverbs 13:4 (NCV)

The Bible tells us that a lazy person hates work, loves sleep, gives excuses, wastes time and energy, and is a fool. God created us to work, not to sit around doing nothing! We become a burden to other people when we are lazy. "Anyone who does not provide for their relatives, and especially for their own household, has denied the faith and is worse than an unbeliever" (1 Timothy 5:8 NIV). Christians are not saved by their works, but they do show their faith by their works.

- Laziness sometimes results in poverty. "Work brings profit, but mere talk leads to poverty!" (Proverbs 14:23 NLT). When able-bodied people refuse to work, this places a burden on our society and creates unnecessary poverty.
- Laziness creates dependence upon others. "You yourselves know that these hands of mine have supplied my own needs and the needs of my companions" (Acts 20:34 NIV). The apostle Paul was a tentmaker, and he supported himself with his trade. Paul did not work to become rich, but to be free from being dependent on anyone else.
- Laziness promotes foolishness. "Go watch the ants, you lazy person. Watch what they do and be wise. Ants have

no commander, no leader or ruler, but they store up food in the summer and gather their supplies at harvest" (Proverbs 6:6-8 NCV). Lazy people do not prepare for the future but expect other people to always help them. God expects us to always be prepared.

- Laziness destroys society. "A lazy person is as bad as someone who destroys things" (Proverbs 18:9 NLT). We see many U.S. cities that have been destroyed because of lazy people. We definitely should not promote laziness in our country. If we continue to give people free handouts, they will not learn to work. This is never good because these people become slaves to the government.

Christians should definitely avoid laziness! We must remember that God created us to work. "The Lord God took the man and put him in the Garden of Eden to work it and take care of it" (Genesis 2:15 NIV). Work is a gift from God and a way to glorify Him; when we work hard, we are a positive testimony to others.

The lazy person who loves sleep
Will not have a harvest to reap.
The lazy person who depends on others
Creates a burden for his sisters and brothers.
The lazy person who wastes time
Will not have a productive lifetime.
The lazy person must learn to get work done
In order to have a fruitful life in the long run.

Lighten Your Load with Laughter

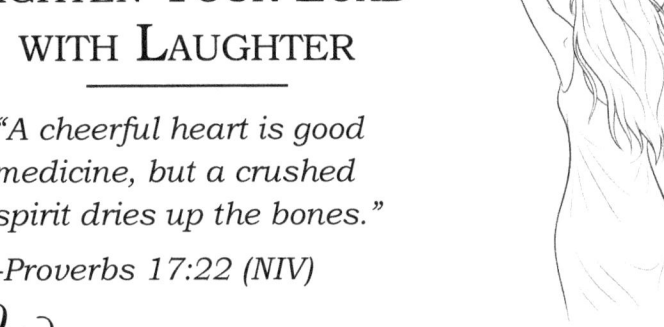

*"A cheerful heart is good
medicine, but a crushed
spirit dries up the bones."*

-Proverbs 17:22 (NIV)

When we were children, we laughed hundreds of times a day, but when we became adults, we succumbed to the burdens of our "to-do" lists. We need to continue laughing and filling our hearts with joy because laughter is the best medicine!

The medicinal benefits of laughter have been documented throughout history. In the 1300s, Henri de Mondeville, a French surgeon, incorporated laughter into the healing process. He believed that his patients would heal more quickly if their family members and friends told them jokes and tried to cheer them up. In the 16th century, Robert Burton, an English minister, used humor when he counseled people suffering from depression. He encouraged these people to surround themselves with others who could make them laugh. During the polio outbreak in the 1930s, many hospitals used clowns to cheer up sick children.[1] Laughter is free medicine that benefits your physical health in many ways.

- Laughter boosts the immune system by decreasing stress hormones and increasing immune cells. It is your natural way to improve resistance to diseases.
- Laughter triggers the release of endorphins, the body's nat-

ural feel-good chemicals. Endorphins promote an overall sense of well-being and can even temporarily relieve pain.

- Laughter protects the heart. Laughter improves the function of blood vessels and increases blood flow, which can help to protect you from a heart attack.

Not only is laughter great for your physical health, but it also benefits your mental health.

- Laughter reduces stress and anxiety. Laughter reduces levels of cortisol, the stress hormone, leading to a state of relaxation.
- Laughter strengthens relationships. Sharing laughter adds joy and vitality, and it unites people during difficult times.
- Laughter causes you to focus on the positive. It is impossible to be in a bad mood when you are laughing.

A life filled with laughter is a good life. When we choose to laugh, play, and have fun, life is more enjoyable. We cannot always choose what happens to us, but we can choose our attitude toward each situation. Sometimes a good laugh can alleviate some of the pain and misery in our lives. "A miserable heart means a miserable life; a cheerful heart fills the day with song" (Proverbs 15:15 MSG). Laughter is the best medicine, and the Great Physician's prescription tells us to have cheerful hearts.

Laugh and have a smile on your face,
So you can spread joy all over the place.
When you smile rather than frown,
You show that suffering will not bring you down.
Laughter is the best medicine for your heart,
Because sadness and sorrow will soon depart.
Laughter is the best medicine for your soul;
It is prescribed by the Great Physician to make you whole!

LOVE AT ALL TIMES

*"A new commandment I
give to you, that you love
one another, even as I
have loved you, that you
also love one another."*

-John 13:34 (MEV)

*L*ove can help us ease our burdens, because when we truly love others, we are not focused on ourselves. And the less we focus on ourselves, the more likely we are to forget about our own problems. We are to love others based on Jesus' sacrificial love for us. Love is more than warm feelings; it is an attitude that reveals itself in action. When we love other people, we help them, even when it is not convenient for us. This kind of love is difficult, but it is the kind of love that Christians should demonstrate to the world.

People have always turned to music for inspiring songs about love, and it is estimated that over 100 million love songs have been recorded. Whitney Houston told us, "I Will Always Love You," and Elvis Presley sang, "Can't Help Falling in Love." Millions of singers have given us their take on love, but the best advice on love is found in God's Word.

"Love is patient, love is kind. It does not envy, it does not boast, it is not proud. It does not dishonor others, it is not self-seeking, it is not easily angered, it keeps no record of wrongs. Love does not delight in evil but rejoices with the truth. It always protects, always trusts, always hopes, always perseveres" (1 Corinthians 13:4-7 NIV). Most of us have heard this passage of Scripture at weddings. When the bride and groom recite these words, they may not understand how difficult love can be. True love demands loving when we do not "feel" like loving. Each part of this passage describes how we are to love others.

- "Love is patient, love is kind." Patience is not easy in our fast-paced society. Patience challenges us to slow down and accept differences in other people and not give up on them.
- "Love does not boast." Selfishness is part of our human nature. We notice this in our "selfie" society that begins sentences with the word "Me and my friends" instead of "My friends and I." (Not only is this incorrect grammatically, but it is also an indication of who is first in someone's life.)
- "Love does not keep a record of wrongs." When you love someone, you should toss out the scorecard because you are not looking for a winner! Love always wins!
- "Love rejoices with the truth." If you are seeking the truth, do not listen to the media—whether it be Hollywood media, social media, or news media. These sources do not supply the truth about love. Turn to your Bible for the truth.

When God commands us to love others, it is not an option! Even when we do not "feel" like loving others, we must still love. If we truly love God, we will love others!

We should show God's love to one another
Because in Christ we are a sister and a brother.
When God's love is in our heart,
Then loving others is doing our part.
True love will always win,
And joy and peace will begin.
When we live a life filled with love,
We know that it is sent from Heaven above.

M

MEND WHAT YOU CAN—GIVE THE REST TO GOD

*"He heals the
brokenhearted and binds
up their wounds."*

-Psalm 147:3 (NIV)

$\mathcal{S}$ometimes we keep things that we think we will fix or repair at some time in the future. Our junk drawers are full of these broken gadgets! Sometimes we waste our precious time trying to mend something that is beyond repair. We should simply throw away, recycle, or donate unwanted items because someone else may have the expertise to fix these broken things.

Everyone is not an expert in every field. We rely on coaches to lead us to victory, but only God can give us a victorious life. We depend on contractors to build our homes, but only God promises us mansions in Heaven. We count on surgeons to perform heart surgery, but only God can mend a broken heart. So, how does God mend a broken heart?

- "The Lord is close to the brokenhearted and saves those who are crushed in spirit" (Psalm 34:18 NIV). God is always with us in the midst of our heartbreak. We may be grieving the loss of a loved one, and we feel that our heartbreak will never end, but God promises to be close to us in our suffering. He will never leave us nor forsake us when we are in the valley of death.

- "My flesh and my heart may fail, but God is the strength of my heart and my portion forever" (Psalm 73:26 ESV). Sometimes, God allows us to endure suffering and sorrow in order to strengthen our hearts. When we walk through the hard times in life, we know that we are not alone—God is with us, and He is making our hearts stronger every day.

- "Peace I leave with you; my peace I give you. I do not give to you as the world gives. Do not let your hearts be troubled and do not be afraid" (John 14:27 NIV). With Christ's peace, we have no need to fear anything—present or future. The peace offered by the world is usually defined as the absence of conflict; however, the peace that Christ gives us is a confident assurance in any circumstance. When we have peace, our hearts will not be troubled.

- "Let not your hearts be troubled. Believe in God; believe also in me" (John 14:1 ESV). After the Last Supper, before Jesus was arrested, He comforted His disciples by assuring them that His death would not be the end. He told them that they would be able to overcome any trials and temptations they faced with the Holy Spirit's help. We should not allow our hearts to be troubled because we know that the same spirit that raised Jesus from the dead lives within us.

Jesus takes our broken heart and repairs and restores it. He mends it and makes it brand new. Even though we may be great at mending broken gadgets in our junk drawers, Jesus is the only one who can mend a broken heart!

God can mend every broken heart.
We must trust in Him for a fresh start.
He will comfort us in times of sorrow,
And we will find our hearts better tomorrow.
He will deliver us from our heartbreak,
And the pain and suffering, He will take.
When we trust in God and believe,
A mended heart is what we will receive.

MODIFY YOUR MINDSET

*"Do not conform to the
pattern of this world, but
be transformed by the
renewing of your mind.
Then you will be able to test
and approve what God's
will is—his good, pleasing
and perfect will."*

-Romans 12:2 (NIV)

God has good, pleasing, and perfect plans for us. He wants us to be transformed people with renewed minds, living to honor and obey Him. Our refusal to conform to the world's values must be firmly planted in our minds, or we will succumb to Satan's traps. "The god of this age has blinded the minds of unbelievers, so that they cannot see the light of the gospel that displays the glory of Christ, who is the image of God" (2 Corinthians 4:4 NIV).

The gospel is open and revealed to everyone, except those who refuse to believe. Satan is the "god of this age." His work is to deceive, and he has blinded those who do not believe in Christ. The allure of possessions, power, and pleasure blinds people to the light of Christ's gospel. Those who choose to reject Christ have unknowingly made Satan their god. We see this in all of the evil that is rampant in our world. We see this in the lifestyles of people who will do anything to make more money. We see this in the false religions and secular philosophies that have brainwashed millions of people.

Throughout history, cults have brainwashed people with their charismatic leaders. One cult leader who promised his followers a utopia in the jungles of South America was Jim Jones. He declared himself the messiah of the Peoples Temple, and he convinced his 900 followers to commit suicide by drinking poisoned Kool-Aid. This tragic mass suicide became known as the Jonestown Massacre.[1]

We wonder how so many people could be so foolish! But we must remember that we cannot modify our mindsets simply by relying on our own power. We must rely on Jesus to combat the false views of the world. "For the weapons of our warfare are not of the flesh but have divine power to destroy strongholds. We destroy arguments and every lofty opinion raised against the knowledge of God, and take every thought captive to obey Christ" (2 Corinthians 10:4-5 ESV). We are in a spiritual warfare, and we are powerless against the devil's tactics.

We must not let the false beliefs of this world modify our mindsets. We must decide to be on the winning team and follow God, not Satan. God wants us to choose Him, but He has given us the power to make our own choices. We do not want to become mindless robots that do not possess critical thinking and will end up in a scrapyard. We are human beings who will spend an eternity either in Heaven or hell. Our mindset should be to choose life—not death! "Today I ask heaven and earth to be witnesses. I am offering you life or death, blessings or curses. Now, choose life! Then you and your children may live" (Deuteronomy 30:19 NCV).

We must modify our mindset,
Or the enemy will become a threat.
If we listen to what the world tells us,
Then we are not following Jesus.
We must rely on God's power,
Which is available to us every hour.
If we choose to follow the enemy,
Our minds and souls will not be free.

MOVE FORWARD—
NOT BACKWARD

*"Look straight ahead,
and fix your eyes on
what lies before you."*

-Proverbs 4:25 (NLT).

Imagine walking backwards for 8,000 miles! This is what Plennie Lawrence Wingo (1895-1993) did! He walked backwards from Santa Monica, California, to Istanbul, Turkey, from April 15, 1931, to October 24, 1932. He remains the Guinness World record holder for "greatest extent of reverse pedestrianism." Wingo hoped his feat would secure him fame and fortune; however, he faced many setbacks along his journey. In order to accomplish his feat, he used sunglasses with rear-view mirrors, but they did not always prevent accidents from occurring. When Wingo was traveling through Ohio, he stepped into a hole and broke his ankle, which resulted in a three-week hospital stay. When he was traveling across the ocean, he suffered from seasickness. When he finally arrived at the Turkish border, he was arrested and thrown in jail. Wingo accomplished a remarkable feat, but he did not earn the fortune he hoped for! When he ended his journey, he had only $4 in his pocket.[1]

Most of us would not attempt to walk backwards for 8,000 miles, but some of us choose to walk backwards through life by dwelling on our past mistakes, regrets, and problems. This is not the life that God wants us to live. "Forget the former things; do not dwell on the past" (Isaiah 43:18 NIV). God wants us to move forward as Ruth did in the Bible.

Ruth's story is one of hope and a brighter future. Ruth had married the son of an Israelite family while they were living in Moab, but when her husband, father-in-law, and her husband's only brother died, Ruth had a difficult decision to make. She had to choose whether to stay in Moab, her home, or to go with her mother-in-law, Naomi, to a land she had never known. Naomi encouraged her daughters-in-law, Ruth and Orpah, to stay in Moab and start their lives over. Orpah agreed, but Ruth loved Naomi and chose to follow her to Israel. "But Ruth replied, 'Don't urge me to leave you or to turn back from you. Where you go I will go, and where you stay I will stay. Your people will be my people and your God my God'" (Ruth 1:16 NIV).

Although Ruth belonged to a race often despised by Israel, she was blessed because of her willingness to follow Naomi and move forward with her life. She believed that there were better days ahead, and she believed that her past was not her final destination. She became a great-grandmother of King David and a direct ancestor of Jesus!

Another woman in the Bible did not move forward; she looked back. Before God destroyed the city of Sodom for its wickedness, He sent an angel to warn Lot, his wife, and his daughters to flee from the city and not look back. However, Lot's wife did not flee; she hesitated and looked back at the fire that was destroying the city, and then she was destroyed.

God wants us to move forward—not backward! He offers us a brighter future than what we had in the past, and He makes promises to us that will last. If we keep going forward, we will find a better life!

We must fix our eyes on the road ahead;
Then we will have nothing to dread.
If we choose to walk backward,
Our journey will be deterred.
So we must not dwell on the past,
Or we will be downcast.
When we move forward, our future is bright;
We just need to keep God in our sight!

N

Notice God's Magnificent Creation

"For ever since the world was created, people have seen the earth and sky. Through everything God made, they can clearly see his invisible qualities—his eternal power and divine nature. So they have no excuse for not knowing God."

-Romans 1:20 (NLT)

*W*hen my husband and I took a trip to Yellowstone National Park, we were in awe at the magnificence of God's creation. There is so much beauty to be found in Yellowstone's 2.2 million acres, including 500 active geysers, 67 species of mammals, 285 species of birds, 290 waterfalls, and 1,000 miles of hiking trails.[1] Exploring God's beautiful national park gave us time to reflect on the divine nature of God. Through nature, God teaches us, speaks to us, and provides for us.

- What does nature teach us? "But ask the animals, and they will teach you, or ask the birds of the air, and they will tell you. Speak to the earth, and it will teach you, or let the fish of the sea tell you. Every one of these knows that the hand of the Lord has done this. The life of every creature and the breath of all people are in God's hand" (Job 12:7-10 NCV). Nature is God's marvelous masterpiece. With every brush stroke of God's hand, He created beauty where nothing existed.

- How does nature speak to us? "The heavens proclaim the glory of God. The skies display his craftsmanship. Day after day they continue to speak; night after night they make him known. They speak without a sound or word; their voice is never heard. Yet their message has gone throughout the earth, and their words to all the world" (Psalm 19:1-4 NLT). The beauty of nature is a universal language that transcends barriers and speaks to all people. No matter where someone lives, there is beauty to be found in nature.

- How does nature provide for us? "You make the grass for cattle and vegetables for the people. You make food grow from the earth" (Psalm 104:14 NCV). God provides for us through everything He created. Our job is to care for nature and be good stewards. We should not be wasteful or destructive; we should try to preserve God's magnificent creation.

Through the ages, people have been inspired by God's gift of nature. In the spring of 1863, Folliott Sandford Pierpoint (1835-1917) sat on a hilltop outside of Bath, England, admiring the majestic view of the Avon River and the countryside filled with primroses and violets. He praised God for the marvelous gift of nature in his hymn "For the Beauty of the Earth."[2]

> For the beauty of the earth,
> For the glory of the skies,
> For the love which from our birth
> Over and around us lies.
> Christ, our Lord, to you we raise
> This, our hymn of grateful praise.[3]

When we marvel at God's creation,
Our souls are filled with elation.
When we see nature's magnificent display
Each and every day,
We are in awe of God's design
And in His creation that is divine.
God has given us nature's beauty,
So being good stewards is our duty.

Nourish Your Soul

"What good will it be for someone to gain the whole world, yet forfeit their soul? Or what can anyone give in exchange for their soul?"

-Matthew 16:26 (NIV)

We try to make our physical bodies last as long as possible by keeping hydrated and eating healthy food. Who knows? We may live to be 100 years old by adhering to a healthy lifestyle. However, our souls will live longer than 100 years—our souls are eternal. Therefore, they need proper nourishment. Just as a steady diet of junk food leads to many health problems and diseases, a steady diet of the junk of this world leads to a diseased soul.

Our souls become diseased when we follow the world's perspectives on life. When we choose to ignore God's Word and follow the world's advice, then we fill our souls with food without nourishment. "People do not live by bread alone, but by every word that comes from the mouth of God" (Matthew 4:4 NLT). Knowing Bible verses nourishes our souls and helps us resist the devil's attacks, but we must also obey the Bible. Jesus was able to resist all of the devil's temptations because He not only knew Scripture, but He obeyed it. The devil knew Scripture, but he did not obey it. In our corrupt world, it is easy to forfeit our souls because of the lies that the devil tells us. The lies of the world try to tempt us to forsake God in order to gain the power, possessions, and pleasures which the world offers. But these things are only temporary—our souls are not!

135

Our souls will live forever, either in the presence of God in Heaven or in punishment in hell. The souls that reject God's love are condemned to pay for their own sin, eternally, in hell. "For the wages of sin is death, but the gift of God is eternal life in Christ Jesus our Lord" (Romans 6:23 NIV). Why would anyone choose to reject God's free gift of eternal life with Him? Many people simply believe that this short span of time on Earth is all there is. They have become conditioned to believe that "living for today" is all that matters. Society has become lax in teaching people that a loving God is also a just God who exacts punishment. Death has a "sting" for those who do not believe in God. "Where, O death is your victory? Where, O death, is your sting? The sting of death is sin, and the power of sin is the law. But thanks be to God! He gives us victory through our Lord Jesus Christ" (1 Corinthians 15:55-57 NIV). Christians do not fear death because Jesus overcame death when He rose from the grave!

Our ephemeral bodies house our eternal souls, and our eternal souls need to be nourished. "And now, dear brothers and sisters, one final thing. Fix your thoughts on what is true, and honorable, and right, and pure, and lovely, and admirable. Think about things that are excellent and worthy of praise" (Philippians 4:8 NLT). If you are not feeding your soul with the Word of God, you are feeding it with something else! You must always nourish your soul.

If you forfeit your soul,
Your life will not be whole.
If you reject God's gift of life,
You will suffer much strife.
If you seek the world to gain,
You will be filled with much pain.
So nourish your soul every day;
Read God's Word and pray.

Number the Great Things God Has Done

"The Lord has done great things for us, and we are filled with joy."

-Psalm 126:3 (NIV)

In our self-absorbed society, it seems that fewer people express thankfulness. Handwritten thank-you notes should be sent for gifts received for special occasions, such as weddings, bridal and baby showers, graduations, and anniversaries. These thank-you notes should also be mailed in a timely manner—not six months later! Lack of time should not be an excuse for writing thank-you notes. Remember that the gift-giver invested more time in giving the gift, when you take into account time spent working in order to pay for the gift, selecting and wrapping the gift, and going to the special occasion! Even though we live in a digital age, a simple text or email is not an appropriate expression of gratitude for special occasion gifts!

God has given us the greatest gift of all—eternal life with Him. "For God so loved the world that he gave his one and only Son, that whoever believes in him shall not perish but have eternal life" (John 3:16 NIV). We should express our gratitude by praising God every day! "This is the day that the Lord has made; we will rejoice and be glad in it" (Psalm 118:24 MEV). We should be thankful every morning, every day, and every evening. We should always be thanking and praising God! We did not do anything to deserve God's marvelous gift that He has lavished upon us. "For it is by grace you have been saved, through faith—and this is not from yourselves, it is the gift of God" (Ephesians 2:8 NIV).

When we consider all of the wonderful blessings that God has bestowed upon us, our hearts should be filled with gratitude. A literary character who was always grateful was Pollyanna. In the novel *Pollyanna*, written by Eleanor H. Porter, eleven-year-old Pollyanna Whittier is sent to live with her stern aunt after the deaths of her missionary parents. Aunt Polly Harrington is not overly happy to raise her niece; she is simply fulfilling her moral obligation.

Pollyanna's outlook on life is to find something positive in every situation. She learned to be optimistic from her father, who taught her to play the "glad game." This game originated one Christmas when Pollyanna thought she would find a doll in the donation box for her family; however, a pair of crutches was the only thing left in the box. Her father taught her to be glad for the crutches because she was able to walk without using them. When Aunt Polly forced Pollyanna to live in a stuffy attic, she marveled at the beauty outside the attic window. Pollyanna eventually inspired the people around her to be thankful. Even though some people might think that Pollyanna was unrealistic or overly optimistic, she was not. She was simply taught to see the silver lining in every situation.

There is a silver lining in every situation if we choose to find it. We can choose to be stern and sullen like Aunt Polly or be joyful and jubilant like Pollyanna. When we number all of the great things God has done, our hearts should be full of joy and jubilation!

Every day God gives us so much to be thankful for;
He supplies us with what we need and so much more.
He lavishes us with gifts from everyone,
But the most important gift is His Son.
So we should have hearts full of gratitude,
And heartfelt thankfulness should be our attitude.
When we try to be thankful in every situation,
Then our hearts are filled with gratitude and elation!

OFFER KINDNESS—NOT CRUELTY

"Those who are kind benefit themselves, but the cruel bring ruin on themselves."

-Proverbs 11:17 (NIV)

*D*o you want to be remembered as a kind person or a cruel person? Most of us would say "kind." Therefore, we must demonstrate kindness by our actions.

- One person who has been remembered for her kindness was Mother Mary Joseph Dallmer, an Ursuline Sisters nun. When a hurricane hit Galveston, Texas, in 1900, it killed nearly 12,000 people, destroyed 3,600 homes, and almost wiped out the town of Galveston. This hurricane is still considered the deadliest hurricane in U.S. history. During this disaster, Mother Mary Joseph opened the doors of the Ursuline Academy to 1,000 refugees. Mother Mary Joseph and the other nuns used their own food and clothing for the refugees, and they risked their lives rescuing people from the floodwaters.[1]
- Another person remembered for an act of kindness following a tragedy was Harold Lowe. He was the only officer aboard the *Titanic* to return to the shipwreck to search for survivors. He rescued four people from the frigid waters of the Atlantic Ocean. When the *Titanic* sank on April 15, 1912, over 1,500

people lost their lives. Officer Harold Lowe is remembered for his act of kindness and bravery.[2]

- A person who showed kindness to the Jews in World War II was Oskar Schindler, who was a German industrialist and humanitarian. Schindler protected 1,200 Jews who worked in his factories from the Nazis. In order to prevent his workers from being sent to concentration camps, he spent most of his life savings on bribes to the Nazi officials.[3]

Even though we may never be known worldwide for our acts of kindness, someone will remember us for the kindness which we lavished upon them, because we never truly know the impact which our kindness has upon other people. Simple words of kindness are beneficial to everyone. "Kind words are like honey—sweet to the soul and healthy for the body" (Proverbs 16:24 NLT).

How is kindness healthy for your body? It can increase self-esteem, empathy, and compassion, and improve your mood. It can also decrease blood pressure and stress. Kindness can change your brain by boosting levels of serotonin and dopamine, which are neurotransmitters that produce feelings of satisfaction and well-being. Endorphins, your body's natural painkillers, also may be released when you show kindness. Kindness is good for your overall health, and being kind may also help you live longer.

Rather than bombard people with cruelty, we should shower them with kindness. Instead of speaking words of hate, we should inspire others with words of hope. When kindness becomes our way of life, we eliminate a lot of strife!

When we choose to be kind—not cruel,
Then we practice the Golden Rule.
We should be kind every day
In everything we do and say.
We should be kind to everyone we meet,
And offer encouraging words to all we greet.
When we keep kindness in our soul,
Then we can show God's love wherever we go.

OPPOSE THE ONSLAUGHT OF EVIL

"Therefore put on the full armor of God, so that when the day of evil comes, you may be able to stand your ground, and after you have done everything, to stand."

-Ephesians 6:13 (NIV)

$\mathcal{E}$vil is prevalent in our world today! Murder, rape, human trafficking, and terrorist attacks are often in the news. How can we fight against evil? Only with the armor of God! Satan will continue his malicious attacks on Christians until Christ returns, so we must put on the full armor of God every day. "Finally, be strong in the Lord and in his mighty power. Put on the full armor of God, so that you can take your stand against the devil's schemes. For our struggle is not against flesh and blood, but against the rulers, against the authorities, against the powers of this dark world and against the spiritual forces of evil in the heavenly realms" (Ephesians 6:10-12 NIV).

This passage of Scripture clearly tells us that our battle is spiritual—not physical. We cannot physically see our enemy, but we see the havoc Satan continues to wreak on our world. Because Satan wants to destroy as many lives as he possibly can, we must be dutiful and dedicated in our commitment to God, and we must diligently put on all of the armor that God supplies.

- "Stand firm then, with the belt of truth buckled around your waist, with the breastplate of righteousness in place" (Ephesians 6:14 NIV). Satan fights with lies, and sometimes lies sound like the truth. We are fed lies every day by people in power, so we must depend upon the belt of truth to protect us and the breastplate of righteousness to guard our hearts.

- "And with your feet fitted with readiness that comes from the gospel of peace" (Ephesians 6:15 NIV). The terrain was rocky in the ancient world, requiring sturdy, protective footwear, and on a battlefield, the enemy might scatter barbed spikes or sharp stones to slow an army down. Satan scatters traps as we try to spread the gospel.

- "In addition to all this, take up the shield of faith, with which you can extinguish all the flaming arrows of the evil one" (Ephesians 6:16 NIV). The soldier's shield fended off arrows, spears, and swords. Our shield of faith guards us against Satan's poisonous arrows of doubt, discouragement, and dismay.

- "Take the helmet of salvation and the sword of the Spirit, which is the word of God" (Ephesians 6:17 NIV). The helmet protects our thoughts from the evil thoughts of our enemy. The sword of the Spirit is the only offensive weapon in our faith arsenal, and we need to fight back at Satan with God's Word.

Finally, we must pray. Every soldier knows that he must keep his lines of communication open with his commander. Ephesians 6:18 (NIV) tells us to "pray in the Spirit on all occasions."

Evil is prevalent in our world today,
So we must put our armor on and pray.
The enemy shoots poisonous arrows at our heart,
But God's strong shield will tear them apart.
God's armor helps us every hour,
And God keeps us safe with His mighty power.
We know that God will have the final victory,
And we will be safe from the enemy and free!

ORGANIZE YOUR LIFE

"But let everything be done in a right and orderly way."

-1 Corinthians 14:40 (NCV)

$\mathcal{I}$ love being organized! All of my cabinets, closets, and cupboards are organized in my home, and I find that being organized saves money, helps with time management, and reduces stress.

- Organizing saves money. When you look in your cupboard and see that you already have ten cans of tomato soup, maybe you do not need more, unless you have a large family or you are stockpiling for the end of the world! Organizing items in your home keeps you from making unnecessary purchases.
- Organization helps with time management. I organize my closet by the colors of my clothing; therefore, I can quickly choose my outfit for the day. I have also organized my husband's closet and my parents' closets. My husband has his tools organized in his garage, which saves time. If a person is constantly trying to find items, they are wasting time and perhaps money. People sometimes purchase items they already have, simply because they could not find them. I also organize my day. I devote my early morning to studying the Bible. This helps me be more productive the rest of the day. After Scripture reading, I am encouraged to accomplish more items on my to-do list.

- Organization reduces stress. When you can quickly find items, you feel less stress. Before I go to bed each night, I have all the items I need for the next day laid out on my kitchen table. I also taught my daughters to do this when they were in school, so our mornings would be less stressful.

When we are organized, we are able to do everything God wants us to do. We should feel a sense of urgency in accomplishing all that needs to be done in our lives, so we should strive to be organized. "We must quickly carry out the tasks assigned us by the one who sent us. The night is coming, and then no one can work" (John 9:4 NLT).

A Biblical character who quickly accomplished what God laid upon his heart to do was Nehemiah. He left a comfortable and wealthy position in Persia to return to his homeland and rebuild Jerusalem's wall. He made a plan, got his resources, divided the workload, and inspired others to help in the rebuilding project. Even though Nehemiah faced opposition as he was working, he finished the wall in fifty-two days! Nehemiah's organizational skills and hard work were necessary in completing a seemingly impossible task. Before we undertake any project, we must assess our resources and get organized. "For who among you; intending to build a tower, does not sit down first and count the cost to see whether he has resources to complete it?" (Luke 14:28 MEV).

If you want to save money, time, and reduce stress in your life, get organized!

If you organize your life,
You will have less chaos and strife.
You will have more time to get things completed,
And you will not feel defeated.
If you seek organization each day,
You will find it is a better way.
When you get organized and make a plan,
You will find God will help you do what you can.

PACK AWAY YOUR PRIDE

"Pride leads to destruction; a proud attitude brings ruin."

-Proverbs 16:18 (NCV)

Foolish pride always brings us down and always places a heavy burden upon us. Satan was cast out of Heaven because of pride, and he will be cast down to hell in the final judgment of God. People who place themselves on a pedestal have a long way to fall!

Pride has kept many people from accepting Jesus as their Savior. Prideful people refuse to admit their sins and refuse to acknowledge that they need Christ in their lives. These people forfeit eternal life in Heaven because they rely on their foolish pride. "The Lord hates those who are proud. They will surely be punished" (Proverbs 16:5 NCV).

Pride is giving ourselves the credit for something that God has accomplished. Anything we accomplish in this world would not be possible if God did not enable us and sustain us. It is so humbling to see world-class athletes give God glory for their accomplishments! Whether these athletes had God-given talent or an amazing work ethic, God had a hand in their achievements, as He does in every- thing worthwhile that any of us accomplish in life.

What happens when we fail to recognize how much God has done for us? We become braggarts! "Who says you are better than others?

What do you have that was not given to you? And if it was given to you, why do you brag as if you did not receive it as a gift?" (1 Corinthians 4:7 NCV). When we become braggarts, we may tumble and fall and lose it all! This happened to King Nebuchadnezzar in the Bible. He was so full of himself that he declared, "Look at this great city of Babylon! By my own mighty power, I have built this beautiful city as my royal residence to display my majestic splendor" (Daniel 4:30 NLT). Immediately, God told Nebuchadnezzar that he no longer ruled his kingdom, and he was sent to live like a wild animal for seven years. Finally, Nebuchadnezzar let go of his pride, acknowledged God, and regained his kingdom.

God gives us life and the ability to live an abundant life in Him. When we begin to believe that we are better than other people and worship ourselves rather than God, then we cause our own destruction. "If anyone thinks he is important when he really is not, he is only fooling himself" (Galatians 6:3 NCV). The story of the Pharisee and the tax collector in the Bible gives us an excellent example of the foolishness of pride. When the self-righteous Pharisee prayed in the temple, he bragged that he followed religious rules, and he thanked God that he was not as bad as the tax collector. However, the tax collector prayed for God to have mercy on him because he was a sinner. Jesus said, "I tell you that this man, rather than the other, went home justified before God. For all those who exalt themselves will be humbled, and those who humble themselves will be exalted" (Luke 18:14 NIV).

We must remember that sinful pride is not the same as striving to have a good self-image, and sinful pride is not the same as taking pride in our work. The sin of pride is an attitude of independence from God, ungratefulness to God, and thinking that we are better than other people. Sinful pride always leads to destruction.

When we succumb to our foolish pride,
We allow the enemy to be our guide.
When we begin to think we are always better,
Then we allow pride to become a fetter.
When we brag that we are number one,
We fail to give credit to God's Son.
When we set ourselves up above all,
Our pedestal topples, and we have a long way to fall.

PRAISE GOD IN THE STORMS

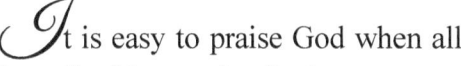

"I will praise the Lord at all times; his praise is always on my lips."

-Psalm 34:1 (NCV)

It is easy to praise God when all is well with your family, but can you still praise God when you lose your family? Horatio Spafford, writer of the famous hymn, "It Is Well with My Soul," continued to praise God even in the midst of tragedy.

Horatio and Anna Spafford were blessed with a wonderful family and a comfortable lifestyle. But tragedy struck their family in 1871 when the Great Chicago Fire destroyed most of the Spafford's real estate investments. Two years later, in 1873, Horatio decided to take Anna and their four daughters on a trip to England. Before their ship set sail, Horatio had to take care of urgent business; therefore, his wife and daughters sailed on ahead without him. Tragically, the ship they were traveling on was struck by another ship, and 226 people lost their lives, including the Spafford's four daughters. Miraculously, Horatio's wife, Anna, survived. When Horatio was sailing to England to meet his wife, he wrote his beautiful hymn "It Is Well with My Soul."[1]

> When peace, like a river, attendeth my way,
> When sorrows like sea billows roll;
> Whatever my lot, Thou hast taught me to say,
> It is well, it is well with my soul.[2]

I cannot imagine suffering the loss of my children, and I pray that this never happens! But I also pray that I would be able to praise God and say, "It is well with my soul."

We will all undergo suffering in life, whether it is the loss of family members, debilitating illnesses, or perhaps the destruction of our homes. But when we can praise God in the storms of life, we reap many benefits.

- Even in the storms of life, we know that God protects us. "But let all who take refuge in you rejoice; let them sing joyful praises forever. Spread your protection over them, that all who love your name may be filled with joy" (Psalm 5:11 NLT).
- When we go through deep waters, God is with us. "When you go through deep waters, I will be with you. When you go through rivers of difficulty, you will not drown. When you walk through the fire of oppression, you will not be burned up; the flames will not consume you" (Isaiah 43:2 NLT).
- We know that the storms of life will pass. "Yet what we suffer now is nothing compared to the glory he will reveal to us later" (Romans 8:18 NLT).

When a tornado almost destroyed our home, I knew that God was protecting us, that He was with us, and that the storm would pass! I praised God because He kept us safe, even though parts of our home were damaged.

If we praise God during the storms of life, we focus more on Him rather than the storms raging around us. When we set our hopes on our future life, we realize that the storm clouds will pass away, and we will see a brighter day!

If we can praise God in the storm,
We will find we are not forlorn.
If we can praise God when the waters are deep,
We will find His promises He will keep.
If we can praise God when tragedy is in our way,
We will find we are not filled with dismay.
If we can praise God when sorrow surrounds us,
We will find hope and comfort in Jesus.

PRAY MORE—PANIC LESS

"Never stop praying."

-1 Thessalonians 5:17 (NLT).

"Never stop praying" does not mean that we spend our days on our knees; it means that we have an attitude of prayer at all times. We have the privilege of being in constant communication with God throughout our days. We may pray formally, quickly, or silently. Our prayers may be eloquent or simple! The main thing we do when praying is to speak from our hearts without overthinking what is in our heads because God is more interested in what is in our hearts—not the words in our heads.

We must remember that our prayers may not be answered during our lives; we see this in the life of William Tyndale (1494-1536), an English biblical scholar who believed that everyone in England—from the king to the servants—should have access to the Bible written in English. Therefore, Tyndale began translating the Bible from the original Hebrew and Greek into English, even though this was a crime punishable by death. On October 6, 1536, William Tyndale was hanged, and his body was burned. However, before he died, he prayed, "Lord, open the king of England's eyes." Two years after Tyndale's death, his dying prayer was answered. King Henry VIII decreed that a copy of the Bible written in English would be in every church in England.[1]

Another man who prayed fervently was George Müller (1805-1898), who founded schools and orphanages while serving as a missionary in Bristol, England, in the 1800s. As a pastor, Müller decided to live without a salary. He prayed that God would move people's hearts to supply his family with what they needed. He then decided to build an orphanage, so he prayed fervently, and in eighteen months, he had enough money for his building project. Müller continued to rely on prayer to supply the daily needs of the orphanage. One morning, the housemother of the orphanage informed Müller that there was no food. The children were told to go into the dining hall and sit at the tables, where Müller gave thanks for the nonexistent food. Within minutes, there was a knock on the door. A baker told Müller that he could not sleep during the night, so he got up early and baked three extra batches of bread for the orphanage. Then there was another knock on the door. A milkman's cart had broken down in front of the orphanage, and the milkman told Müller that the milk would spoil before the cart was fixed, so the milkman gave ten large cans of milk to the hungry children. Over the years, donations poured in for the orphanage, which eventually housed more than 10,000 children.[2]

George Müller did not panic—he prayed. He believed that God would provide what was needed. His prayers demonstrated his faith in God. We need to be like Müller and truly believe that God hears our prayers and that God will provide what we need. "Therefore I tell you, whatever you ask for in prayer, believe that you have received it, and it will be yours" (Mark 11:24 NIV). God wants us to pour out our hearts to Him and truly seek Him. "Then you will call on me and come and pray to me, and I will listen to you. You will seek me and find me when you seek me with all your heart" (Jeremiah 29:12-13 NIV). Because God is the only one who truly knows our hearts, we can be totally honest with Him. Prayer is so powerful because we are communicating with the Creator of the Universe!

Prayer empowers what we do and say;
So we must fervently pray every day.
Prayer's supernatural power
Can change situations every hour.
God may not answer us right away,
But we know He hears us if we pray.
When we pray more and panic less,
We find that our lives are forever blessed.

Q

QUELL THE QUARRELS IN YOUR LIFE

"It is to one's honor to avoid strife, but every fool is quick to quarrel."

-Proverbs 20:3 (NIV)

*S*ometimes foolish quarrels can evolve into legendary feuds. Such is the case of the Hatfield-McCoy feud, which lasted from 1863 to 1891, with the official end occurring when family descendants signed a formal truce in 2003.

The Hatfields were headed by "Devil Anse" Hatfield, and the McCoys by "Randall" McCoy, each of whom fathered thirteen children. The Hatfields lived in Logan County, West Virginia, and the McCoys were from Pike County, Kentucky, and the two families lived on opposite sides of a border stream, the Tug Fork. How did these two families get into a lengthy feud? Some people believe the feud between the two families began in the Civil War because the Hatfields were Confederates and the McCoys fought for the Union. Other people think the feud started when a Hatfield stole a hog from the McCoys. No matter how the feud started, it continued with occasional fights until 1882, when Ellison Hatfield was killed by some of the McCoys in a brawl. To avenge Ellison's murder, the Hatfields kidnapped and executed three McCoy brothers—Tolbert, Phamer, and Randolph, Jr. After that incident, the two families repeatedly ambushed and killed one another, and it is estimated that between twelve and fifteen Hatfields and McCoys eventually lost their lives.[1]

As we learn from the Hatfield-McCoy feud, it is better to quell quarrels before they escalate into tragedy and needless destruction. "Whoever loves a quarrel loves sin; whoever builds a high gate invites destruction" (Proverbs 17:19 NIV). Also, if we allow anger towards someone to fester in our hearts, we allow the devil to take hold of our lives. "In your anger do not sin: Do not let the sun go down while you are still angry, and do not give the devil a foothold" (Ephesians 4:26-27 NIV). A foothold is a great thing when climbing a mountain; it allows the climber to securely scale the mountain. However, we need to avoid giving the devil a secure foothold in our lives. That is why we must deal with anger before it deals with us.

We all have felt anger when we have been unfairly treated or when we have been wronged by others. But we must not seek revenge, like the Hatfields and McCoys did. This only exacerbates anger and causes it to ooze into a seeping wound in our hearts. It is also better to avoid foolish arguments. "Don't have anything to do with foolish and stupid arguments, because you know they produce quarrels" (2 Timothy 2:23 NIV).

If we are to quell the quarrels in our lives, we must not allow anger to control us. "My dear brothers and sisters, take note of this: Everyone should be quick to listen, slow to speak and slow to become angry" (James 1:19 NIV). This is sometimes difficult to do; however, it would be more problematic to engage in a foolish feud than to deal with anger!

It is better to quell a quarrel before it starts;
If not, anger can fester in your hearts.
If you start a feud and are a fool,
You give the devil a chance to rule.
So do not allow anger to control your life,
Or you will be filled with bitterness and strife.
You should strive to live in peace with everyone,
And then you will be blessed by God's Son!

QUIT YOUR QUEST FOR MORE STUFF

"Then he said to them, 'Watch out! Be on your guard against all kinds of greed; life does not consist in an abundance of possessions.'"

-Luke 12:15 (NIV)

*W*ho needs 3,000 pairs of shoes? Imelda Marcos apparently did! Imelda Marcos became First Lady of the Philippines in 1965, when her husband, Ferdinand Marcos, was elected as the country's 10th president. Imelda served as First Lady for more than twenty years, and during this time, she was known for her extravagant lifestyle during a period of economic crisis in her country.

Imelda's massive shoe collection became a symbol of excess in a country where many people walked barefoot because of poverty. It is believed that the Marcos family embezzled billions of dollars from the country's coffers, and the Marcos regime became known for its oppressive rule. Ferdinand Marcos eventually declared martial law in 1972, basically making himself the country's dictator.[1] The lavish lifestyle of Imelda became known worldwide. On her most famous shopping spree, Imelda spent $7 million in 90 days during a 1983 trip to New York, Rome, and Copenhagen. Imelda and her husband were eventually driven into exile in the U.S. after a 1986 people's revolt.[2]

Accumulating more stuff never satisfies anyone. If it did, then King Solomon, the richest king the world has ever known, would have found joy in everything he owned. However, he expressed the futility of material possessions when he declared, "Those who love money will never have enough. How meaningless to think that wealth brings true happiness!" (Ecclesiastes 5:10 NLT). The belief that more material possessions will lead to happiness is a lie fed to us by the enemy. Materialism creates many problems in our lives.

- Materialism ends in ultimate futility. After King Solomon's years as the world's richest man, he said, "Yet when I surveyed all that my hands had done and what I had toiled to achieve, everything was meaningless, a chasing after the wind; nothing was gained under the sun" (Ecclesiastes 2:11 NIV).

- Materialism promotes injustice and exploitation. The Marcos regime exploited the poor people in the Philippines. "If anyone has material possessions and sees a brother or sister in need but has no pity on them, how can the love of God be in that person?" (1 John 3:17 NIV).

- Materialism causes us to rely on earthly treasures, which do not last. Part of the massive shoe collection of Imelda Marcos was eventually destroyed by termites, weather, and neglect. "Do not store up for yourselves treasures on earth, where moths and vermin destroy, and where thieves break in and steal. But store up for yourselves treasures in heaven, where moths and vermin do not destroy, and where thieves do not break in and steal" (Matthew 6:19-20 NIV).

- Materialism obscures many of the best things in life, which are free—including the gift of salvation. Money cannot buy salvation, and it cannot rescue us from judgment. "Riches will not help when it's time to die, but right living will save you from death" (Proverbs 11:4 NCV).

We must quit the quest for more stuff
Because it does not satisfy and is never enough.
If we believe that our treasures on Earth
Will last forever and are of worth,
Then we will accumulate things that do not last,
And we will always be sad and downcast.
The only treasure we should seek
Is God's eternal love, which we can keep.

QUOTE GOD'S WORD

*"In the beginning was the
Word, and the Word was
with God, and the Word
was God."*

–John 1:1 (NIV)

*W*hy should we quote God's Word? Because it has always existed, and it will never pass away. "Heaven and earth will pass away, but my words will never pass away" (Matthew 24:35 NIV). According to Guinness World Records, the best-selling book of all time is the Christian Bible. It is impossible to know exactly how many copies have been printed, but research conducted by the British and Foreign Bible Society in 2021 indicates that the total number is between five and seven billion copies. It is estimated that 100 million Bibles are printed each year, and 20 million Bibles are sold each year in the United States! The Bible will continue to surpass all other books because people want to know the truth in a world filled with fake news and false narratives. The Bible benefits us in many ways.

- Reading God's Word helps us encourage other people. "All Scripture is God-breathed and is useful for teaching, rebuking, correcting and training in righteousness, so that the servant of God may be thoroughly equipped for every good work" (2 Timothy 3:16-17 NIV). We should not quote Scripture to other people in order to impress them. The Pharisees in Jesus' day quoted Scripture in order to elevate their status in society rather than to actually help other people. We should share Scripture that tells people about God's love for them.

- Following God's Word helps us become obedient. "Do what God's teaching says; when you only listen and do nothing, you are fooling yourselves" (James 1:22 NCV). The Bible is our guidebook, instruction manual, and road atlas for our lives. When we follow God's instructions, rather than following our own paths, our lives will be better. "Your word is a lamp for my feet, a light on my path" (Psalm 119:105 NIV).

- Quoting God's Word helps us resist temptations. "For the word of God is alive and active. Sharper than any double-edged sword, it penetrates even to dividing soul and spirit, joints and marrow; it judges the thoughts and attitudes of the heart" (Hebrews 4:12 NIV). As a sharp, double-edged sword, the Word of God is our definitive offensive weapon in our spiritual battle against Satan. When Satan tempted Jesus in the wilderness, Jesus quoted Scripture to counter Satan's attacks. We should do the same!

The only way to be ready to quote God's Word is to memorize Scripture. When you do that, you can be a blessing to others. I remember when I was teaching and one of my students asked me why I was so happy. I quickly replied with one of my favorite Scriptures, "This is the day the Lord has made; we will rejoice and be glad in it" (Psalm 118:24 NKJV).

God's Word has endured the test of time,
And it always gives us peace sublime.
God's Word is eternal and will not pass away;
It encourages us when we read what God has to say.
God's Word is our constant guide;
It tells us that God is always by our side.
God's Word can be a blessing to others,
Whether they are strangers, or sisters and brothers.

READ THE "WRITING ON THE WALL"

"So God sent the hand that wrote on the wall."

-Daniel 5:24 (NCV)

The phrase "the writing on the wall" is used to denote that a negative or disastrous event will soon occur. In the book of Daniel, "the writing on the wall" indicated the collapse of the Babylonian empire.

The Babylonian ruler Belshazzar was a wealthy king who gave a banquet for his court. During the drunken party, the sacred vessels that had been stolen from the Jewish temple by Nebuchadnezzar in 586 BC were used in a blasphemous manner. "As they drank the wine, they praised the gods of gold and silver, of bronze, iron, wood and stone" (Daniel 5:4 NIV). Suddenly, a man's hand was seen writing on the wall. King Belshazzar was terrified, and he called on his enchanters, astrologers, and diviners to figure out the meaning of the words "Mene, tekel, and parsin." The men could not interpret the meaning, so the king called in the prophet Daniel, who told him what the words meant.

"This is what the words mean: Mene: God has counted the days until your kingdom will end. Tekel: You have been weighed on the scales and found not good enough. Parsin: Your kingdom is being divided and will be given to the Medes and the Persians" (Daniel 5:26-28 NCV). That very night, Belshazzar was slain and his kingdom passed to Darius the Mede. The Medes and Persians slipped into the city secretly while the Babylonians were at their drunken feast.

The appearance of the "writing on the wall" is a reminder that we reap what we sow. God is the judge, and He justly weighs all matters and metes out retribution in His time. Sometimes, God speaks clearly into our lives, convicting us of sin and warning us of pending judgment, so we should not ignore the "writing on the wall." Even though King Belshazzar had power and wealth, his kingdom was totally corrupt, and he could not withstand the judgment of God. God's time of judgment comes for all people. "For we must all appear before the judgment seat of Christ, so that each of us may receive what is due us for the things done while in the body, whether good or bad" (2 Corinthians 5:10 NIV).

Another corrupt king who should have read the "writing on the wall" was King Ahab. His downfall began when he married the evil Jezebel, who hated God's people and enticed Ahab to worship false gods. She also convinced Ahab to murder an innocent man, so God sent the prophet Elijah to warn Ahab of his impending doom, but Ahab refused to listen. Then God used Ahab's own false prophets to persuade him into going to the battle at Ramoth-Gilead, where he was killed by an arrow and slowly bled to death.

Some people think of God as only loving, not just. These people ignore the teaching of God's judgment in the Bible. "For God will bring every deed into judgment, including every secret thing, whether good or evil" (Ecclesiastes 12:14 MEV). People need to read the "writing on the wall" before it is too late!

If we ignore the "writing on the wall,"
We will experience our downfall.
God's judgment will definitely come,
And it will be for all—not just some.
If God's warnings we do not heed,
It will be a sad day for us indeed.
Even though God is a God of love,
His judgment will rain down from heaven above.

REMEMBER THAT GOD WILL FIGHT YOUR BATTLES

*"The Lord will fight for you;
you need only to be still."*

-Exodus 14:14 (NIV)

When Moses told the Israelites that God would fight for them, they were standing at the edge of the Red Sea with the Egyptian army pressing down upon them. The Israelites thought that there was no way to escape. Then God parted the Red Sea! God may not part a sea for us, but He will fight for us.

Every day, we are battling pride, pressure, and people who want us to rebel against God. When we believe in God and His promises to always be with us in every battle, we avoid panic, fear, and hopelessness. "For the Lord your God is the one who goes with you to fight for you against your enemies to give you victory" (Deuteronomy 20:4 NIV). If we want God to fight for us, then we must listen to what He tells us to do.

Joshua succeeded Moses as Israel's leader, and Joshua is considered one of the Bible's greatest military leaders. The key to his success in battle was his obedience to God. When God spoke, Joshua listened and obeyed. Joshua had to lead more than two million people into a strange land and conquer it. Conquering the land would depend upon Joshua's obedience to God. "Be strong and very courageous. Be careful to obey all the law my servant

Moses gave you; do not turn from it to the right or to the left, that you may be successful wherever you go" (Joshua 1:7 NIV).

Before entering the city of Jericho, God told Joshua that Jericho was already delivered into his hands—the enemy was already defeated. "Then the Lord said to Joshua, 'See, I have delivered Jericho into your hands, along with its king and its fighting men'" (Joshua 6:2 NIV). Then God gave Joshua specific instructions for the battle: march around the city, blow trumpets, and shout. These seemingly ridiculous instructions made it clear to Joshua that winning the battle depended upon faith in God, not upon weapons and military expertise. We all must remember that God has already won the battle and defeated Satan! But sometimes, we have to endure the battlefield!

Sometimes, we may forget how God has fought for us in the past. Joshua told the Israelites how God had faithfully protected them in the past, and he urged the Israelites to remain faithful to God. "But if serving the Lord seems undesirable to you, then choose for yourselves this day whom you will serve, whether the gods your ancestors served beyond the Euphrates, or the gods of the Amorites, in whose land you are living. But as for me and my household, we will serve the Lord" (Joshua 24:15 NIV).

God is our military leader, and He will always fight for us, protect us, and be with us. But if we do not follow His leadership and rely only on our own strength, then we will face the vast armies of despair, discouragement, and defeat on our own. "You will not have to fight this battle. Take up your positions; stand firm and see the deliverance the Lord will give you, Judah and Jerusalem. Do not be afraid; do not be discouraged. Go out to face them tomorrow, and the Lord will be with you" (2 Chronicles 20:17 NIV).

God will fight your battles for you every day,
If you listen to His commands and obey.
God has fought for you in the past,
And His protection is with you and will last.
God will protect you in every future endeavor,
And He will guard you always and forever.
So remember that God is by your side;
Always allow Him to be your guide.

Run Your Own Race

"Therefore we also,
since we are surrounded
by so great a cloud of
witnesses, let us lay
aside every weight, and
the sin which so easily
ensnares us, and let us run with endurance the
race that is set before us."

-Hebrews 12:1 (NKJV)

On May 6, 1954, British athlete Roger Bannister became the first person to achieve what was thought impossible—run a mile in less than four minutes. Runners had been chasing this elusive goal since the late 1800s. Experts thought the four-minute mile barrier would be broken in perfect weather on a particular kind of track in front of a large crowd. However, Roger Bannister achieved the impossible with a time of 3:59.4 on a cold day, on a wet track, at a small meet in Oxford, England, on May 6, 1954. Bannister was a full-time medical student who did not use traditional training methods, and the British press had criticized him for his "lone wolf" approach to running.[1]

Bannister ran the race that was set before him. He was not concerned about what other people thought of his training methods. His main concern was achieving his goal of breaking the four-minute mile, so he kept his eyes set on the finish line.

When we are in the race of life, we must keep our eyes focused on Jesus and our eternal rewards. "Do you not know that in a race all the runners run, but only one gets the prize? Run in such a way as to get the prize" (1 Corinthians 9:24 NIV). What happens when we take our eyes off the finish line? A month after Roger Bannister broke the four-minute mile, John Landy of Australia beat Bannister's record with a time of 3:57.9. After this, the two runners were set to compete against each other at the 1954 Empire Games in Vancouver, Canada. The press called the race "The Miracle Mile." During the race, Bannister and Landy were running close to each other; however, near the finish line, Landy looked back over his shoulder to see where Bannister was, and Bannister passed him to win the race in 3:58.8. Landy finished 0.8 seconds behind him.[2] What would have happened if Landy had kept his focus on the finish line?

When we are running our race, we should not worry about how fast everyone else seems to be going. When we look back, we lose our focus, and we allow our past mistakes to weigh us down. The writer of Hebrews tells us that we must "lay aside every weight" if we are going to run our race with endurance. The athletes in the ancient world stripped off extra weight before participating in a race. Excess body weight was eliminated through strict diets and exercise, and on the day of the race, almost all clothing was stripped off.

What extra things do we need to strip away in order to run the race set before us? Do we need to strip away our doubt and discouragement? Do we need to get rid of our sins that entangle us? Whatever in our lives causes us to lose our focus must be eliminated so we can cross the finish line. "I have fought the good fight, I have finished the race, I have kept the faith" (2 Timothy 4:7 NIV). In order to keep the faith, we must run the race set before us.

When we run the race set before us,
We keep our focus on Jesus.
We do not look back at our past;
We look forward to what will last.
We are not seeking a prize that will perish;
We are running for a reward we will cherish.
When we look forward to the finish line,
We are running for what is divine.

S

Seek Wisdom—Not Wealth

"How much better to get wisdom than gold, to get insight rather than silver!"

-Proverbs 16:16 (NIV)

For many wealthy families, it seems as if their money will never run out! They spend money on lavish vacations, fancy sports cars, and designer clothing. But sometimes money does run out. This is called the third-generation curse, which states that 70% of wealthy families are no longer wealthy by the second generation, and 90% have lost their wealth by the third generation. This is what happened to one of the wealthiest families in America.

The Vanderbilt dynasty began with a hard-working man, Cornelius Vanderbilt (also known as the Commodore). He built an empire, and by the time of his death in 1877, he was the richest man in America. He left the majority of his fortune, valued at $95 million, to his oldest son, William Henry Vanderbilt, and a smaller amount to all of his other children. William doubled his inheritance in the next ten years, creating the largest fortune in the world at that time. However, within a few short years, William's children had spent most of their inheritance.

One of the reasons the grandchildren squandered their money was to keep up with New York high society. The wealthy families of New York did not approve of the Vanderbilt fortune because it was considered "new" money, not "old" money. In order to impress high-class society, Alva Vanderbilt, wife of William Kisson Vanderbilt, and granddaughter of Cornelius Vanderbilt, decided to build the largest mansion in New York City. The mansion took three years to build, costing $3 million, equivalent to $70 million today. Once the mansion was completed, Alva hosted a party, which cost $250,000 ($5.8 million today). Alva thought she finally had the approval of elite society! After this party, other family members built mansions on Fifth Avenue near Alva's home. Unfortunately, those elaborate mansions did not last very long. Alva's mansion, which had been completed in 1882, was demolished in 1927. Her $3 million mansion only lasted 45 years! Not only was her home demolished, but her marriage was, too. Alva and William eventually divorced. When 120 of the descendants of Cornelius Vanderbilt gathered at Vanderbilt University in 1973 for their first family reunion, there was not a millionaire among them.[1]

When we are on a quest for wealth, we must first search for wisdom. There is nothing wrong with being wealthy. Many wealthy people have a great work ethic and are good stewards of their money. However, if these people do not pass on wisdom to the next generations, their families may lose everything. When the third generation is born into a wealthy family and they have never experienced struggles in life, then they may not understand the consequences of extravagant spending. We must teach wisdom, which is only found in God's Word. "Happy is the person who finds wisdom, the one who gets understanding. Wisdom is worth more than silver; it brings more profit than gold. Wisdom is more precious than rubies; nothing you could want is equal to it" (Proverbs 3:13-15 NCV).

Wisdom is something we should seek
If we want our wealth to keep.
Wisdom is reliable and steadfast;
It will guide us to make our money last.
Wisdom is more valuable than silver or gold;
It will pour upon us riches untold.
When we make wisdom our quest,
The wealth it brings will be the best.

SHARE YOUR FAITH

"But my life is worth nothing to me unless I use it for finishing the work assigned me by the Lord Jesus—the work of telling others the Good News about the wonderful grace of God."

-Acts 20:24 (NLT).

One day, when I was picking up my five-year-old granddaughter from pre-K, I asked her, "What did you learn in school today?" She quickly replied,

- "Number one: Love God above everything else."
- "Number two: Don't tell lies."
- "Number three: Don't take anything that belongs to someone else."

I shared my granddaughter's answers with my daughter, and I suggested that she share this with my granddaughter's teachers to let them know what an impact they were making on my granddaughter's life!

When we have good news to share, we want to tell everyone. We tell others when we get engaged, when we are expecting a baby, and when we purchase a new home! But the best news we should share with others is that God loves them! "For God so loved the world that he gave his one and only Son, that whoever believes in him shall not perish but have eternal life" (John 3:16 NIV). God does not want anyone to perish in hell, but some people do not even believe in hell! According to a Gallup poll in 2023, only 59% of Americans believe in hell, even though 67% believe in Heaven.[1] The Bible is clear that if we do not accept Jesus as our Savior, we will spend eternity separated from God! "Whoever believes in the Son has eternal life, but whoever rejects the Son will not see life, for God's wrath remains on them" (John 3:36 NIV).

Because we do not want our family and friends to spend eternity separated from God's love, we should have a sense of urgency in sharing our faith with them. As Christians, we are commanded to tell others how much God loves them. "And he said to them, 'Go into all the world and proclaim the gospel to the whole creation'" (Mark 16:15 ESV). Before Jesus departed to His heavenly throne, He spent time with His disciples and told them to tell others about Him. When we tell other people how Christ has changed our lives, we may not have a dramatic story to tell, but we all have a story. Our story may be how God has been with us through the sunshine and the storms. One story that I tell others is how God protected my family when a tornado hit our house. Every time I share my story, my faith is strengthened.

All we can do is share our faith with other people; it is up to these people to believe. "But in your hearts honor Christ the Lord as holy, always being prepared to make a defense to anyone who asks you for a reason for the hope that is in you; yet do it with gentleness and respect" (1 Peter 3:15 ESV). God's love for us compels us to share our faith with other people. We must remember that God loves everyone, and He does not want anyone to perish, but they will if they do not accept Jesus as their Savior. Therefore, we must share our faith!

We all have good news to share
With family, friends, and strangers everywhere.
God commands us to tell others of His love,
And His saving grace sent from Heaven above.
We do not want anyone to suffer in eternity,
So we let others know how God will set them free.
When we have God's love in our heart,
Then telling others is doing our part!

STOP FOLLOWING THE WRONG PATH

"Ponder the path of your feet; then all your ways will be sure."

-Proverbs 4:26 (ESV)

*W*hy do hikers get lost? If you have ever hiked on well-maintained trails, you might wonder how anyone could get lost. In most cases, people get lost because they wander off the trail. Then they keep forging ahead, thinking that the path they are on is the correct trail. In most cases, hikers should try to retrace their steps if they are lost. Andrew Herrington, a survival instructor, search and rescue team leader, and wildlife ranger in the Great Smoky Mountains, says that anyone can get lost, including experienced hikers. However, of the one hundred search and rescue incidents each year in the Smoky Mountains, 90% are inexperienced day hikers. Some of these hikers are accustomed to relying on GPS to help them navigate city streets; however, they find that GPS is not always reliable in the great outdoors. Herrington says the most important thing hikers should do is to let someone know their itinerary.[1]

It is easy to get lost in our world today. With so many paths to choose from, we mistakenly believe that they are all good. After all, some paths promise exorbitant wealth, beautiful friends, and unending pleasure. Wealth, friends, and pleasure are not bad things; however, the path we travel to find these things may make us lose our way. Along this path, what sacrifices will we need to make, how far will we have to travel, and what is our final destination? A person would not aimlessly hike through the woods without knowing where the trail would take them. In our lives, we need to make sure we are on the trail that leads to a good destination, not a bad one. If we want to make sure we are on the right path, we must follow what Jesus says: "Enter through the narrow gate. For wide is the gate and broad is the road that leads to destruction, and many enter through it. But small is the gate and narrow the road that leads to life, and only a few find it" (Matthew 7:13-14 NIV).

The road that leads to eternal life is open to everyone, but many people keep following the wrong path. Following Jesus is not easy, and when faced with the choice between traveling a narrow, bumpy road and gliding on a wide, paved highway, most people opt for the easier road. Most of us like comfort and pleasure, and Satan has paved the highway to hell with alluring attractions that try to divert us from the best path to follow.

Some people believe that their prestige, possessions, and power will guarantee them a spot in heaven. However, Jesus says, "I am the way and the truth and the life. No one comes to the Father except through me" (John 14:6 NIV). Some religions and famous people try to profit by offering false ways to salvation, but there is no other way except through Jesus Christ.

We should not be like hikers who get lost and continue going on the wrong path. In life, it may seem that we are too far gone down a path to ever find our way home. But the Bible tells us, "For the Son of Man came to seek and to save the lost" (Luke 19:10 NIV). We should not be too proud to admit that we need help getting back on the right path in life, and we should stop following the wrong path!

If the wrong path is what you follow,
You may end up with a life that is hollow.
If you find that you are lost,
You must change your direction to avoid a high cost.
You should not follow a path that leads to destruction;
Instead, you should follow God's instruction.
Sometimes, you need to get on a better road
That ends up in blessings upon you bestowed.

TRADE YOUR TURMOIL FOR TRUST

"Trust in the Lord with all your heart; do not depend on your own understanding. Seek his will in all you do, and he will show you which path to take."

-Proverbs 3:5-6 (NLT)

*B*ecause God is always trustworthy, He will always lead us on the right paths in life. Trusting in God definitely makes it easier for us to navigate our way through the turmoil in life. So why should we trust God?

- We can count on God to always be with us. We will experience unexpected hardships in our lives, and it is in these times that our trust is tested. But the only way to get through the turmoil in our lives is to trust in God. When Shadrach, Meshach, and Abednego chose not to bow down to King Nebuchadnezzar's golden statue, they knew the penalty was death; however, they trusted God regardless of the consequences they faced. God may not always intervene on our behalf, but we know that He will never forsake us. "Those who know your name trust in you, for you, Lord, have never forsaken those who seek you" (Psalm 9:10 NIV).

- We can learn to trust others when we first trust God. Trust is foundational to human relationships, but not all people are trustworthy. More than likely, our trust will be broken at some point in our relationships. King David was betrayed many times by people close to him, and he expressed his feelings when he stated, "It is better to trust the Lord than to trust people" (Psalm 118:8 NCV). However, David learned a valuable lesson: sinful people will fail us, but we can always trust in God.

- We do not have blind trust. Just because a particular teaching appears to have authority or popular acceptance does not mean it is biblically sound. While we should submit to our leaders, we cannot blindly trust everything we hear from sources of supposed authority. We sometimes wonder why anyone would trust evil people. Adolf Hitler used his position of authority to bring out the evil in his followers, getting everyday people to commit atrocities. When people do not trust in God first, then it becomes easier for them to blindly trust in people. "Blessed is the man who makes the Lord his trust, who does not turn to the proud, to those who go astray after a lie!" (Psalm 40:4 ESV).

Many people live in a constant state of turmoil because they mistakenly trust in every new idea, influencer, or idiot who is popular! We must remember that God alone is always trustworthy. He always keeps His promises, always answers our prayers, and always protects us every day. So, trade your turmoil for trust!

When we trust in God to lead us through,
We find He is with us in all we do.
Our trust in God makes us depend,
And we know His promises never end.
We should trust in God above all
Because He will never allow us to fall.
We can trust in God every day
Because He will be with us along the way.

TREASURE THE TRUTH

"The very essence of your words is truth; all your just regulations will stand forever."

-Psalm 119:160 (NLT)

"*D*o you swear or affirm, under penalty of perjury, that the testimony you are about to give is the truth, the whole truth, and nothing but the truth, so help you God?" We all know the importance of telling the truth in a courtroom proceeding, especially if someone's life is on the line. But all of our lives are on the line if we do not know the truth!

So, what is truth? By definition, truth is "conformity to fact or actuality; a statement proven to be or accepted as true." Truth is *not* simply whatever works. Lies can appear to "work," but they are still lies and not the truth. Truth is *not* what makes people feel good because bad news can be true. Truth is *not* what the majority says is true. A majority of people can believe a lie. Some people think that truth is narrow-minded. However, truth *is* narrow; for example, two plus two always equals four. There is no other answer.

Why is absolute truth important? Because life has consequences when we do not adhere to the truth. If we believe a bottle of poison is not really poison, and we drink it, we will die. If we jump off a tall building, not believing in gravity, then we will suffer serious injury or death. The most significant consequences of ignoring truth are seen in a person's faith. Jesus said, "I am the way and the truth and the life. No one comes to the Father except through me" (John 14:6 NIV). Not adhering to this truth has eternal consequences—eternity separated from God!

Truth cannot depend on "situational ethics," the belief that what is right or wrong is relative to the situation. This leads to a "whatever feels good" mentality and lifestyle, which has devastating effects on society and individuals. If there are no absolutes, then chaos ensues. If there is no absolute truth, then there is nothing ultimately right or wrong about anything. People would be free to do whatever they want—murder, rape, steal, or lie—and no one could say those things are wrong. Absolute truth is necessary for harmony to exist in society.

Some people believe that adhering to the truth results in a loss of freedom; however, the opposite is true. Following the truth sets us free. "Then you will know the truth, and the truth will set you free" (John 8:32 NIV). Jesus Himself is the truth that sets us free. He is the source of truth, the perfect standard of what is right. He frees us from continued slavery to sin, from self-deception, and from deception by Satan, who is the father of lies. Jesus shows us clearly the way to eternal life with God. Jesus does not give us freedom to do what we want, but freedom to follow God.

It is imperative that we know the truth in our society today because we are constantly bombarded with opinions posing as the truth! We must remember that opinions constantly change! Children hold onto the opinion that candy is good for them. Teenagers have the opinion that they know what is best for them. As mature adults, we need to look beyond opinions and seek the truth!

When we follow the truth each day,
We know that Jesus is the only way.
Following Jesus' truth sets us free
Even though some people may not agree.
The enemy tangles the truth in order to deceive,
But we know the truth of Jesus is what we believe.
When we have the truth of Jesus in our heart,
Then the enemy's lies will soon depart.

TURN AWAY FROM EVIL

"Do not set foot on the path of the wicked or walk in the way of evildoers. Avoid it, do not travel on it; turn from it and go on your way."

-Proverbs 4:14-15 (NIV)

*B*ecause we live in a fallen world filled with many temptations, it is very easy to follow the path of the wicked. This path is best avoided by never starting on it, because once you are on an evil path, it takes effort to get off of it. The wickedness in the world tries to lure you in with its seductive power. Hollywood often celebrates sin, advertisers sometimes promote unhealthy lifestyles, and social media may condone evil behavior.

We must remember that Satan is the god of this world, and he has his own value system contrary to God's. We cannot be a friend of the world and be able to resist the path of the wicked. "So, you are not loyal to God! You should know that loving the world is the same as hating God. Anyone who wants to be a friend of the world becomes God's enemy" (James 4:4 NCV). The world consists of people whose beliefs, values, and morals are in direct opposition to God. We must be careful not to deceive ourselves into thinking we can live in close fellowship with God and, at the same time, set our hearts on things of the world.

In order to avoid the path of the wicked, we must resist the devil. "Therefore submit yourselves to God. Resist the devil, and he will flee from you" (James 4:7 MEV). Although God and the devil are at war, we know that God has already defeated Satan. Satan is here now, and he is trying to win us over to his evil regime. With the Holy Spirit's power, we can resist the devil. We can allow Satan to have authority over us and follow his evil path, or we can follow God. We can resist the devil by reading and studying God's Word, by praying throughout the day, and also by using common sense, which tells us to avoid bad situations and evil people.

Throughout history, people have been led astray by following evil leaders. Adolf Hitler used propaganda aimed at exploiting the German people and telling them lies. The people were told that Jews were their enemies and, therefore, they should be destroyed. People may be blinded to the path of evil and attracted to an evil leader's charisma and confidence. Some people may succumb to peer pressure and not question an evil leader's motives, and other people may follow evil leaders for personal gain. Whatever the reasons are, we must not follow the path of evil!

Hindsight is always better than foresight; therefore, we should reflect upon the lessons learned from history and not choose to follow the path of evil. The propaganda used today is much more sophisticated than what was used in the Nazi era, so we must be vigilant in not being swayed by popular views and persuasive news. Every day, we must decide which path we will set foot on. Is it the path purported by the media to be the best one? Or is it the reliable path revealed to us in God's Word?

We must avoid evil and turn away,
Or it will cause us to go astray.
The path of evil will deceive,
And cause us not to believe.
If evil destroys our heart,
It will take over and not depart.
So we must resist the wicked one,
And turn instead to God's Son.

U

UNPACK YOUR PROBLEMS

"Then call on me when you are in trouble, and I will rescue you, and you will give me glory."

-Psalm 50:15 (NLT).

*W*hat happens when you do not unpack your dirty clothes from your suitcase? Sweat and dirt provide a breeding ground for bacteria to grow, causing a strong, musty odor. Stains become set-in and are more difficult to remove. The dark, enclosed space of the suitcase can attract pests like moths, which may lay eggs on your clothes. Mold can begin growing on your clothes in twenty-four hours, and any clean clothes in your suitcase will become contaminated from your dirty clothes! Unpack your suitcase!

We need to unpack our problems and give them to God. If we keep our problems packed up inside of us, they will continue to get worse and eventually contaminate all of the joy in our lives. Everyone suffers from problems, but God promises to always be with us.

- "God is our refuge and strength, an ever-present help in trouble" (Psalm 46:1 NIV). Because we live in a fallen world, we experience heartache and pain. We witness disasters and depravity. We suffer from diseases and depression. Wars rage, and peace eludes our world. But God will not fail to rescue those who love Him. God is not merely a temporary refuge; He is our eternal refuge, and He can provide us strength to help face any circumstance. God does not promise to remove our problems from us, but to protect us during our difficulties.

- "You have allowed me to suffer much hardship, but you will restore me to life again and lift me up from the depths of the earth" (Psalm 71:20 NLT). None of us likes to suffer hardships, but they are a part of life. And sometimes our problems can perfect us, just like fire refines metal. When we walk through the fires of life with God by our side, then we are strengthened. We know that God will restore us in eternity.

- "Though I walk in the midst of trouble, you preserve my life. You stretch out your hand against the anger of my foes; with your right hand you save me" (Psalm 138:7 NIV). God is actively involved in the lives of those who depend on Him, even when they are facing adversity. As Christians, we should expect continuing tension with an unbelieving world. But when we give our problems to God, He comforts us and will not abandon us. Even though the enemy is always trying to attack us, we know that he has already been defeated. He is like a soldier who continues to fight a battle, not knowing that the war has already been won.

We should seek God's help when we face difficulties because God hears us and understands our needs. Our problems do not have to become our permanent predicament. We should unpack our problems and give them to God!

If we keep our problems packed in our soul,
We do not give God the chance to make us whole.
Our problems will fester and contaminate;
They will harm us and stagnate.
So we must rely on God to help us out;
He will restore us, without a doubt.
When we give our problems to our Father above,
He will strengthen us with His unfailing love.

Unplug Every Day

"Yes, my soul, find rest in God; my hope comes from him."

-Psalm 62:5 (NIV)

$\mathcal{O}$ne of the first things many of us do each morning is to check our phones. We want to see what we may have missed, check birthdays for the day, find out the weather forecast, or check out a Scripture of the day. All of these things can be good; however, we may find it necessary to unplug from technology so we can plug into God.

To point out how dependent we are on technology, consider the following statistics: There are over 6.8 billion smartphone users in the world, and 6.3% of these users have a cell phone addiction. Also, according to a 2024 survey, 50% of Americans spend 5-6 hours on their smartphones every day.[1] Spending too much time on social media can create a multitude of problems. When a person receives social media notifications, such as "likes" or comments, the brain may increase dopamine levels. Dopamine is a hormone responsible for feelings of pleasure, and the more time spent on social media, the more likely a person is to become addicted to it, just as someone can become addicted to gambling or drugs.

Social media is useful for many things; however, when we unplug from it occasionally, we find many benefits.

- Our self-esteem will improve. If we spend too much time focused on the "picture-perfect" lives of other people, we forget how blessed we are. We will never be satisfied with our own lives if we seek constant approval from other people. Instead, we should focus on God's approval. "Therefore do not throw away your confidence, which has a great reward" (Hebrews 10:35 ESV).

- Our mental health will improve. Spending too much time on social media can cause feelings of loneliness, depression, envy, jealousy, and dissatisfaction, and many people are plugged into their phones 24/7, which creates tension and stress in their lives. We need to put down our phones and quiet our lives. "Teach me, and I will be quiet. Show me where I have been wrong" (Job 6:24 NCV).

- Our physical health will improve. Spending excessive time sitting in front of screens can lead to a sedentary lifestyle and various health issues. Your brain, eyes, neck, hands, arms, and back can all experience strain. You need to get up, go outside, and spend time in God's creation in order to rejuvenate your life. "You will go out in joy and be led forth in peace; the mountains and hills will burst into song before you, and all the trees of the field will clap their hands" (Isaiah 55:12 NIV).

- Our sleep and rest will improve. The blue light emitted by screens can disrupt our natural sleep patterns and negatively impact the quality of our rest, which can cause many health issues. "I go to bed and sleep in peace, because, Lord, only you keep me safe" (Psalm 4:8 NCV).

We need to unplug every day, so we can plug into God!

We need to unplug from our phones to find rest
Because too much screen time can make us depressed.
If we rely on social media for our identity,
We will not be filled with peace and serenity.
If we allow social media to take over our life,
We will suffer from continual strife.
When we unplug from the world every day,
We can plug in to God's blessings along the way.

Unwrap Your Unique Gifts

"In his grace, God has given us different gifts for doing certain things well. So if God has given you the ability to prophesy, speak out with as much faith as God has given you."

-Romans 12:6 (NLT)

Of the 8.2 billion people in the world, no two people are exactly identical, not even identical twins. Even though identical twins share many physical characteristics, each twin has unique fingerprints. God created each individual as a unique person with unique gifts and abilities. If you ever feel unimportant, unloved, or unappreciated, remember how special you are!

- "For we are God's handiwork, created in Christ Jesus to do good works, which God prepared in advance for us to do" (Ephesians 2:10 NIV). Everything that God creates is of value, yet nothing in creation compares to God's work in creating mankind. Each individual is intricately and uniquely created by God; we are unique masterpieces with our own set of gifts, abilities, and characteristics. No masterpiece designed by human hands can compare to us! Perhaps you have seen the painting *Mona Lisa*, which is considered one of the greatest masterpieces of all time. Did God send His

208

Son to the cross to die for this painting? Definitely not! God loves you and cares for you because you are His masterpiece!

- "I praise you because I am fearfully and wonderfully made; your works are wonderful, I know that full well" (Psalm 139:14 NIV). God's character goes into the creation of every person. When you feel worthless or begin to hate yourself, remember that God's spirit is within you. The human body is the most complex and unique organism in the world, and that complexity tells us about our Creator. Every aspect of the body reveals that it is fearfully and wonderfully made. The human brain has the ability to learn, reason, and control many functions of the body, to maintain balance to walk, run, stand, and sit, all while concentrating on something else. Computers can outperform the brain in calculating power, but are slower when it comes to performing most reasoning tasks.
- "Before I formed you in the womb I knew you, before you were born I set you apart; I appointed you as a prophet to the nations" (Jeremiah 1:5 NIV). God knew you, as He knew Jeremiah, long before you were born or even conceived. He thought about you and planned for you. You are not an accident! When you feel discouraged or inadequate, remember how valuable you are to God, and remember that He has a purpose in mind for you.

We are God's masterpiece, workmanship, and handiwork! Despite the imperfections we see in ourselves, God knows what He is doing. He has given each person unique qualities and unique gifts. Imagine how boring the world would be if everyone had an identical appearance and similar gifts! So unwrap your unique gifts and see how wonderful you are!

You are God's unique masterpiece,
And your value will never decrease.
You are God's wonderful design,
Created by the hands of the divine.
You are God's magnificent work of art,
And He instilled magnificence in your heart.
So remember that God used His amazing love,
When He created you from heaven above!

V

VALUE EVERY MOMENT

"Teach us to number our days, that we may gain a heart of wisdom."

-Psalm 90:12 (NIV)

*N*ow that I am in the 4th quarter of my life, I think more about the brevity of life. I reflect upon the average life expectancy in the United States, which is 75 years for men and 80 years for women. Neither my husband nor I is at those ages quite yet, but we will be sooner than we think. I wonder if I will live to be 100 years old or older! On December 29, 2024, Tomiko Itooka of Japan passed away at the age of 116 years old. She lived a long life, but she did not set a record. According to Guinness World Records, Jeanne Louise Calment of France lived 122 years 164 days, and she was active her entire life, being able to walk without assistance until her 115th birthday! This is remarkable!

Whether a person lives to be 100 years old or not, life is still short! We should live our lives focused on things that matter—things that have eternal significance. We should be filled with a sense of urgency in ensuring that our loved ones have accepted Jesus as their Savior and that they are not putting off until tomorrow this important decision! We may foolishly believe that we are in control of the time clock—but we are not. Our lives are not a ballgame where the referee can add more time to the clock! The clock keeps ticking whether we want it to slow down or not!

In the book of James, we are told, "But you do not know what will happen tomorrow! Your life is like a mist. You can see it for a short time, but then it goes away" (James 4:14 NCV). No one is guaranteed tomorrow. In the past few years, I have attended more funerals than at any other time in my life. Why? Because my friends and loved ones are getting older, just like me. We should not be deceived into thinking that we have plenty of time in our lives to live for Christ, to enjoy our loved ones, or to complete tasks that need to be done.

None of us knows how much time is left on our clocks. But we know for sure that they will eventually stop ticking! Therefore, we should live with eternity in mind—an eternity spent with God. We should not waste our precious time doing things that will not matter. On average, people spend three hours per day watching television and two hours per day scrolling through social media. But what about spending time in God's Word? Unfortunately, only 11% of adults read their Bibles every day!

We should realize that we are writing our obituaries every day. Do we want our obituaries to read, "This person amassed significant wealth, owned several mansions and fancy sports cars, and was a member of many organizations"? Or do we want our obituaries to say, "This person passed from this life to his/her eternal home"? Because our lives are fleeting, we must make the most of our days. "Show me, Lord, my life's end and the number of my days; let me know how fleeting my life is" (Psalm 39:4 NIV).

In the blink of an eye, our time on Earth will come to an end. The time clock cannot be reset. The hourglass cannot be turned over. We cannot turn back time!

Today may be your last day on Earth,
So how do you measure your time and worth?
Will it be by the amount of money you have earned,
Which can be stolen, lost, or burned?
Will it be by the acquisition of power,
Which can be lost in an hour?
Will it be by your popularity and fame,
Which will not always remain?
Hopefully, you will value every day
And cherish the time you have along the way!

VEER OFF THE POPULARITY PATH

"Do you think I am trying to make people accept me? No, God is the one I am trying to please. Am I trying to please people? If I still wanted to please people, I would not be a servant of Christ."

-Galatians 1:10 (NCV)

When we seek our validation and self-worth from the opinions of other people, we are on the wrong path. We need to veer off the popularity path because popularity is an elusive god that many people have chased to their own destruction.

Consider fad diets, which typically promise weight loss in a short amount of time. These diets usually do not teach sustainable eating habits, and they can be potentially dangerous to a person's overall health. Many of these diets are endorsed by popular celebrities who probably do not follow the diets themselves. Another popular trend, especially among young women today, is spending exorbitant amounts of money on skin care. We definitely need to care for our skin, but we should not purchase products simply because of celebrity endorsements.

We must remember that popular opinion changes quickly, sometimes daily, and when we place too much importance on it, we are creating a heavy and expensive burden for ourselves. We will easily become disappointed when we see that the money we spent on the latest trend is wasted because the trend is no longer a trend. When we try to find our personal worth in anything or anyone besides God, we are destined for disappointment. A focus on popularity is an obsession with self. We cannot consistently please both God and the world. People may love us or hate us, but when we choose to allow God to define our value rather than other people, we free ourselves from the burden of trying to please other people.

The desire to be popular and famous can seem overwhelming because it seems that the popular people have everything! But we have Jesus as a great example of how we should live. After Jesus fed 5,000 people, the people wanted to make Him king. "When Jesus saw that they were ready to force Him to be their king, He slipped away into the hills by Himself" (John 6:15 NLT). Jesus had the opportunity to be famous, but He knew that this was not His Father's plan. A desire for fame and popularity is not wrong in itself, if we will use our fame as a worldwide platform to glorify God, but that is sometimes difficult to do. Think of how many popular singers and actors could glorify God with their talent, but they choose not to.

Everyone who desires to be popular will have to choose many times between the approval of others and the approval of God, and God's plan for us is often in conflict with the world's plan for us. To be "popular," we must choose the world, but doing so means Jesus is not the Lord of our lives. "Do not love the world or the things in the world. If you love the world, the love of the Father is not in you" (1 John 2:15 NCV).

We must remember that the latest fad will fizzle out and be forgotten. The newest trend will be tossed out with the trash, and the opinions of popular people will pass away. So, we must veer off the popularity path and steer toward a pleasing path to God!

The popularity path promises success and fame,
But sometimes failure and loss are what you gain.
If you count on popularity to last,
You will become discouraged and downcast.
Do not buy into the latest fad;
You will become disappointed and sad.
Do not follow the latest trend;
Follow Jesus whose presence will never end.

VITALIZE YOUR FAITH

"And without faith it is impossible to please God, because anyone who comes to him must believe that he exists and that he rewards those who earnestly seek him."

-Hebrews 11:6 (NIV)

When we earnestly seek God, He rewards our faith in Him by bestowing His many blessings upon us. There have been many faithful Christians throughout history, but one man who did not compromise his faith for personal gain was Eric Liddell (1902-1945). Liddell was a devout Christian who ran to glorify God, and he was considered Great Britain's best hope of winning the 100-meter race at the 1924 Paris Olympics. When Liddell learned that the heats for the 100-meter race were scheduled on a Sunday afternoon, he refused to run. His teammate, Harold Abrahams, ended up winning the gold medal in the event. Then Liddell surprised everyone when he won the 400-meter race and set a new world record. After Liddell's Olympic fame, he became a missionary to China. The Olympic feats of Liddell and Abrahams were brought to life in the 1981 movie *Chariots of Fire*, which remains one of the most acclaimed sports films of all time with its iconic soundtrack.[1]

Faith is at the core of Christianity and the Christian life. Genuine faith involves abandoning all human reliance on self-efforts and placing total dependence upon God. The apostle Paul said, "For we walk by faith, not by sight" (2 Corinthians 5:7 MEV). When the world seems to be falling apart, our faith stands secure on the trustworthy promises of God and His Word.

When we stand on the promises of God, we demonstrate our faith. When the disciple Peter stepped out of his boat and walked on water, he had faith. "Then Peter got down out of the boat, walked on the water and came toward Jesus" (Matthew 14:29 NIV). Peter was the only disciple to get out of the boat. But then Peter started to sink in the water because he took his eyes off of Jesus and focused on the waves around him. "But when he saw the wind, he was afraid and, beginning to sink, cried out, 'Lord, save me!' Immediately Jesus reached out his hand and caught him. 'You of little faith,' he said, 'why did you doubt?'" (Matthew 14:30-31 NIV).

We all walk through tough situations in life, and if we focus on the storms around us without looking to Jesus for help, our faith will falter. To vitalize our faith, we must focus on Jesus. When Jesus commands you to do something that may seem impossible, like walking on water, you must obey Him. Faith is taking the next step. The first step may be easy, but you must have faith to keep going. Your "little faith" may become "big faith" when you obey Jesus.

Faith requires us to rely on things that we cannot always see. "Now faith is the substance of things hoped for, the evidence of things not seen" (Hebrews 11:1 NKJV). Would your faith remain strong if you could not see? Many of us are familiar with the hymn writer Fanny Crosby, who became blind at six weeks old. However, Fanny did not let this tragedy weaken her strong faith. She became a teacher at the New York Institute for the Blind, and she eventually wrote 9,000 hymns, with "Blessed Assurance" being one of her most well-known.[2] Even when we cannot see the future, we can all depend upon faith to guide us!

Faith requires us to rely on things we cannot see,
But we know God is with us wherever we may be.
By faith we know upon God we can depend;
Even when we walk through trials we cannot comprehend.
When we have faith, doubt will be removed,
And with faith, our lives will be improved.
In order to vitalize our faith each day,
We must look to God's Word and always pray!

WAIT PATIENTLY ON THE LORD

"The Lord is good to those who wait for him, to the soul who seeks him."

-Lamentations 3:25 (ESV)

one of us likes to wait in our fast-paced society today! With just a click, we seem to have everything we want instantaneously! We can get onto a website within two seconds, with four seconds considered slow. We can deliver a message in seconds. Think about this: in the early 1840s, it took about 180 days for mail to be delivered via wagon trains from New York to San Francisco. In that length of time, news would definitely be old news!

We live in a time where we do not like to wait! Our reliance upon instant gratification seems to have become a part of our prayers and relationship with God. When our prayers are not immediately answered, or when we have to wait too long for something to happen, we lose hope in God. But we must remember that God's timetable is different from ours. Many of us are under a time crunch every day, expecting to have tasks completed within an hour, a day, or a week. Our bosses typically do not say we have years to complete a project. But God is not looking at a calendar and giving us a scheduled time. "Jesus said to them, 'The Father is the only One who has the authority to decide dates and times. These things are not for you to know'" (Acts 1:7 NCV).

Many people in the Bible had to wait many years for God's promises to be fulfilled.

- God promised Abraham that he would be the father of many nations. When Abraham was 100 years old, and his wife, Sarah, was ninety years old, they finally had their son, Isaac.
- Joseph waited thirteen years for his suffering to be redeemed. After being sold into slavery by his brothers and then thrown into prison, Joseph had to wait. Eventually, Pharaoh made Joseph second-in-command in Egypt.
- David had to wait fifteen years from when he was anointed king to when he actually became king.
- When God told Noah to build the ark, Noah was 500 years old. One hundred years later, God flooded the earth.

Instead of focusing on instant results, we must focus on God's timing, which is perfect and precise. The Creator of the universe understands time. "But do not forget this one thing, dear friends: To the Lord one day is as a thousand years, and a thousand years is as one day. The Lord is not slow in doing what he promised—the way some people understand slowness. But God is being patient with you. He does not want anyone to be lost, but he wants all people to change their hearts and lives" (2 Peter 3:8-9 NCV).

In our times of waiting, we learn to rely on God and not ourselves. We discover that we are not in control of every hour of every day. Even though it is good to make plans and be organized, sometimes we have to erase things on our calendars. When things do not go as we planned, we must remember that we can only see a glimpse of the future. God has the master calendar!

We typically do not like to wait
Because we want tasks completed by a certain date.
We get impatient when we must wait an extra hour,
But we must remember time is in God's power.
Our patience is tested if we must wait another day,
But we must remember that God's promises will not fade away.
So learn to wait patiently upon the Lord,
And you will discover God's abundant reward.

WALK AWAY FROM YOUR WORRIES

"Can any one of you by worrying add a single hour to your life?"

-Matthew 6:27 (NIV)

$\mathcal{O}$ne person who could have succumbed to worrying was Corrie ten Boom (1892-1983). Corrie and her family harbored Jews in a secret room above their watch shop in Holland during World War II. They helped over 800 Jews escape, but their efforts were halted when the ten Boom family was eventually arrested. Corrie and her sister Betsie were sent to Ravensbrück concentration camp, where Betsie died in 1944. Corrie was released twelve days later due to a clerical error, and a week after her release, all of the female prisoners from her age group were killed. Corrie told her story in her memoir *The Hiding Place*. One of her famous quotes about worrying was "Worry does not empty tomorrow of its sorrow. It empties today of its strength."[1]

Worrying is nonproductive for many reasons.

- "Therefore do not worry about tomorrow, for tomorrow will worry about itself. Each day has enough trouble of its own" (Matthew 6:34 NIV). Planning for tomorrow is important, but worrying about tomorrow is pointless. Careful planning involves thinking ahead about goals and schedules. When done well, planning can help alleviate worry. Worriers are consumed by fear and find it difficult to trust God.

- "Worry is a heavy load, but a kind word cheers you up" (Proverbs 12:25 NCV). Many of us worry about finances, job security, health and safety of loved ones, our appearance, world events, and death! Worrying about problems never solves them; it only creates more problems. Worrying negatively affects our health and happiness. So, what should we do to cure the problem of worrying? We should delve into God's Word, which is our source of joy in our world of anxiety.

- "So I tell you, don't worry about the food or drink you need to live, or about the clothes you need for your body. Life is more than food, and the body is more than clothes" (Matthew 6:25 NCV). Jesus tells us not to worry about needs that God promises to supply. When we feel overwhelmed with worry, we should pray and thank God for what He has already done in our lives. The more time we spend in prayer, the more peace we will be given, and we may find that our worries disappear. We must remember that God may be challenging us to rely on Him more to provide everything we need—not everything we want!

Remember that time spent worrying is time wasted. Instead of worrying, you should pray about your problems. Instead of fretting about the future, you should focus on today. Instead of bearing the heavy burden of worry, you should lay your concerns at the cross. Remember that God is in control of every second of every day, so let go of your worries and pray!

Don't let worry from the past
Make you feel downcast.
Don't let worry about today
Cause you to lose your way.
Don't let worry about tomorrow
Fill you with sorrow.
If you want worry to disappear,
Remember that God is always near!

WORK WHOLEHEARTEDLY

"Whatever you do, work at it with all your heart, as working for the Lord, not for human masters, since you know that you will receive an inheritance from the Lord as a reward. It is the Lord Christ you are serving"

-Colossians 3:23-24 (NIV)

We are commanded to put forth our best efforts, to work from our hearts and souls at whatever we are doing. We are accountable to God and are stewards of the gifts He has given us; therefore, our work shows our gratitude to God. Christians should work hard because a good work ethic can be a witness to other people, and we never know how many lives we can influence through our dedication to our work.

Two Christian men who were dedicated to spreading the gospel of Jesus Christ were William Booth and Billy Graham. William Booth (1829-1912) was the founder of The Salvation Army. William Booth began his ministerial career in England in 1852, but his compassion for the outcasts of society caused him to abandon the traditional church setting and take his message of salvation to the streets of London. William and his wife, Catherine, began training evangelists throughout England, and within ten years, their organization, known as The Christian Mission, had over 1,000 volunteers and evangelists. William changed the name of their organization to The Salvation Army. This organization brings the message of God's healing and hope to people in over 100 countries.[1]

Another Christian man, Billy Graham (1918-2018), left his legacy to our hurting world. For over fifty-five years, Billy Graham shared the Good News of Jesus Christ with nearly 215 million people in more than 185 countries. Billy Graham was one of the most influential and admired religious leaders of the 20th century. He founded the Billy Graham Evangelistic Association, and his legacy continues through his son, Franklin Graham, who is the President and CEO of Samaritan's Purse, an organization that provides spiritual and physical aid to people throughout the world.[2]

Even if our names are not known worldwide, we all have work to do! "Commit your work to the Lord, and your plans will be established" (Proverbs 16:3 ESV). When we commit our work to the Lord, He will bless our efforts, but the key is "committing" to the Lord! We must acknowledge that God is in control, and we must pray for His guidance in whatever work we do. When we serve the Lord faithfully in our work, then we can leave the results to Him. We may not always have recognition from our employers, but we can count on God to acknowledge our hard work.

What did the wealthy King Solomon say about hard work? "Those who work their land will have plenty of food, but the one who chases empty dreams is not wise" (Proverbs 12:11 NCV). Every honest and useful profession involves hard work. Every business idea that is a get-rich-scheme will fail. When you work, do it with all of your might, and let God take care of the rest. Hard work, self-denial, patience, and God's blessing create success in work. Work hard and faithfully, and God will bestow many blessings upon you!

When we work hard for the Lord,
We will receive a reward.
If we ask the Lord to be our guide,
He will faithfully be by our side.
When we work hard every day,
We can help people along the way.
When we work hard with our whole heart,
The blessings the Lord provides will not depart.

x

X-IRRADIATE THE DARKNESS

"The light shines in the darkness, and the darkness has not overcome it"

-John 1:5 (NIV)

*L*ight shines in the dark, even in the darkest times in history. The Middle Ages in European history, which lasted from the 5th century to the 15th century, were often referred to as the "Dark Ages." During this time period, the Black Death (bubonic plague), which was widespread between 1347 and 1350, killed 20 million people in Europe, and the Hundred Years' War (1337-1453) became an ongoing conflict between the kingdoms of England and France. However, throughout these bleak times, Christianity became the dominant faith in Europe.

After the Roman Empire fell in 476 AD, church structures were not prevalent in cities, so monasteries were established on lands outside of the cities. Monasteries served as centers of Christian worship, with monks dedicated to prayer and spiritual devotion. Monks were often the only literate people in their regions, and they contributed to the spread of Christianity during this dark time in history by copying and distributing the Scriptures. "God once said, 'Let the light shine out of the darkness!' This is the same God who made his light shine in our hearts by letting us know the glory of God that is in the face of Christ" (2 Corinthians 4:6 NCV).

During the Dark Ages, there were many people who became known for their dedication to Christ, and one such person was Joan of Arc (1412-1431). Joan of Arc was an illiterate peasant girl who believed that God had chosen her to lead France to victory during the Hundred Years' War. With no military training, Joan convinced Prince Charles of Valois to allow her to lead a French army to the city of Orléans, the site of an English siege. In a series of battles, the French troops finally took back the city. Joan of Arc was eventually captured by enemy forces, accused of being a witch, and burned at the stake at age nineteen. After her death, her fame increased, and eventually, she was considered one of history's greatest martyrs. She also became the patron saint of France.[1] Joan of Arc was devoted to God, and she let her light shine in the darkness. "In the same way, let your light shine before others, that they may see your good deeds and glorify your Father in heaven" (Matthew 5:16 NIV).

Another person who was a beacon of light during the Dark Ages was Saint Francis of Assisi (1181-1226). In 1202, Francis was captured when fighting in a war between Assisi and Perugia. He was imprisoned, and during this time, he felt that Christ was calling him to live a life of poverty and devote himself to the Church. After being released from prison, Francis devoted his life to helping others, and he became known for his famous prayer.

> Lord, make me an instrument of your peace;
> Where there is hatred, let me sow love;
> Where there is injury, pardon;
> Where there is doubt, faith;
> Where there is despair, hope;
> Where there is darkness, light;
> And where there is sadness, joy.[2]

We all need to become beacons of light and let our love for God shine bright!

The darkness cannot overcome the light,
Because the Lord's light will always shine bright.
When dark clouds get in our way,
We know the Son will shine every day.
When darkness is all around us,
We just need to look to the light of Jesus.
His light shines brightly from Heaven above,
And His brilliance shines bright through His love.

X-out the Stain of Sin

"Though your sins are like scarlet, I will make them as white as snow. Though they are red like crimson, I will make them as white as wool."

-Isaiah 1:18 (NLT)

*M*any of us have seen commercials for cleaning products that will remove stains from carpet. We watch as the stain is magically erased from the carpet, and then we purchase the product and find that it does not completely eliminate the stain! Some stains, such as blood, nail polish, and permanent markers, are nearly impossible to remove if they are not treated immediately!

In Isaiah 1:18, we read that even though our sins are scarlet, they can become as white as snow. In biblical times, scarlet was the color of deep-red permanent dye, and its deep stain was virtually impossible to remove from clothing. Only God can remove the stain of sin from our lives. If we are willing and obedient, Christ will forgive and remove our most indelible stains. We are all in need of cleansing, and the only thing that can wash away our sin is the blood of Jesus!

People must truly repent to have the stains of sin washed away. When Pontius Pilate washed his hands, it was only a symbolic gesture declaring his innocence of his involvement in the death of

Jesus. Pilate thought simply washing his hands would remove his sin! In the William Shakespeare play *Macbeth*, Lady Macbeth also washes her hands. She thinks there is blood on her hands after she manipulated her husband into murdering King Duncan. She felt no remorse for her crime, but she believed that washing her hands would remove the stains of her sin.

When someone truly repents, the stain of sin can be removed. When King David repented of his sins, God mercifully forgave him. King David was truly sorry for his adultery with Bathsheba and for having her husband killed. King David cried out to God, "Wash me thoroughly from my iniquity and cleanse me from my sin!" (Psalm 51:2 ESV). King David wanted the stain of his sin to be removed from his heart. "Create in me a pure heart, O God, and renew a steadfast spirit in me" (Psalm 51:10 NIV). God promises to forgive us of our sins, but He does not always erase the natural consequences of our sins. King David's life and family were never the same as a result of his sins.

All of us are born stained and sinful, and we are all in need of cleansing. We could never use enough cleaning products or quick-fix methods to eradicate our sins. We must repent of our sins and ask Jesus to forgive us. "And you know that Jesus came to take away our sins, and there is no sin in him" (1 John 3:5 NLT). Jesus is the only one who can wash away our sins. The hymn writer Robert Lowry (1826-1899), in his well-known hymn, "Nothing But the Blood," stated that the blood of Jesus is the only thing that will make us "white as snow."

> What can wash away my sin?
> Nothing but the blood of Jesus.
> Oh! Precious is the flow
> That makes me white as snow;
> No other fount I know,
> Nothing but the blood of Jesus.[1]

Only the blood of Christ will free us from sin;
Then our hearts will be cleansed from within.
Only the blood of Christ will make us as white as snow,
Because of Christ's sacrifice, this we know.
Only the blood of Christ will wash away sin's stain,
And then our guilt will not remain.
Only the blood of Christ will purify our heart,
And then our sins will depart.

X-ray Your Heart

*"Above all else, guard
your heart, for everything
you do flows from it."*

-Proverbs 4:23 (NIV)

*B*ecause heart disease is the leading cause of death each year, we know
that we should be proactive in preventing heart disease. According
to the CDC, we should eat a healthy diet with plenty of fruits and
vegetables, be physically active, maintain a healthy weight, refrain
from smoking, limit alcohol intake, manage stress, and get adequate
sleep. If we do not follow these guidelines, we may die from heart
disease.

Taking care of our physical hearts is essential if we want to live
a long, healthy life; however, taking care of our spiritual hearts
is imperative if we want to spend eternity in heaven. Just as our
physical hearts can be attacked by infections, our spiritual hearts can
become infected with sin. When we allow negativity, bitterness, and
anger to take root in our hearts, we allow sin to control our lives.
"For from the heart come evil thoughts, murder, adultery, all sexual
immorality, theft, lying, and slander" (Matthew 15:19 NLT). When
we guard our hearts, we must be vigilant in protecting ourselves
physically, emotionally, and spiritually.

- Physical—If we do not follow a heart-healthy diet, we will
  suffer the consequences. If our diets are filled with ultra-pro-
  cessed foods, our heart health will suffer. Sometimes tasty

238

treats are the worst things for us because they are high in saturated fat, which can raise cholesterol and increase the risk of heart disease. Unfortunately, many delicious foods, such as butter, cakes, biscuits, sausage, bacon, cheese, pastries, and ice cream, contain saturated fat.

- Emotional—If we allow stress to control our lives, we may not get adequate sleep, which is detrimental to our heart health. Sleep is important because it allows our blood pressure to decrease, and sleep may help to control blood sugar levels. Too much stress may also result in unhealthy coping mechanisms like overeating, drinking alcohol, and smoking, which are all bad for our hearts.
- Spiritual—If we allow negative thoughts, excessive pride, and bitterness into our hearts, then we are giving the devil a foothold on our hearts. In order to prevent this, we must actively read God's Word and pray! When we do these things, then God will guard our hearts. "But the Lord is faithful. He will establish you and guard you against the evil one" (2 Thessalonians 3:3 ESV).

We must remember that our hearts are under constant attack from Satan. He is always aiming his poisonous darts at our hearts, so we must focus on what is good, pure, and healthy for our hearts. To protect our hearts, we should pray these words every day: "Let the words of my mouth and the meditation of my heart be acceptable in your sight, O Lord, my rock and my redeemer" (Psalm 19:14 ESV).

We must constantly protect our hearts
Because the enemy is always aiming his poisonous darts.
He tries to penetrate our hearts with evil and hate,
And make us enraged, upset, and irate.
We must not let our spiritual hearts become infected with sin,
By allowing bitterness and anger to fester within.
In order to keep our hearts healthy each day,
We must read God's Word and always pray!

Y

YACK LESS—LISTEN MORE

"Fools care nothing for thoughtful discourse; all they do is run off at the mouth."

-Proverbs 18:2 (MSG)

*W*e all know people who continually yack, yack, yack! They never give others a chance to join in on the conversation because they are constantly talking—talking about themselves, their successes and failures, their possessions and popularity, and anything else on their mind. They have not learned the fine art of listening (truly listening) to other people!

Listening requires us to focus on whoever is speaking to us, and if we adhere to the following habits, we can become better listeners.

- We must resist distractions. We must put our phones down and look at the person who is speaking to us. This enables us to pay attention to the words that are spoken and to be alert to what is not spoken. Sometimes, focusing on body language can give us a better understanding of the true message. "Tune your ears to wisdom, and concentrate on understanding" (Proverbs 2:2 NLT).
- We must suspend judgment, which allows us to hear the entire message before jumping to conclusions. When we truly listen to other people, we may learn something new even if we disagree with their opinions. "Understand this,

242

my dear brothers and sisters: You must all be quick to listen, slow to speak, and slow to get angry" (James 1:19 NLT).

- We must not allow our minds to wander, which is sometimes difficult to do. One of the reasons is that most people talk at a rate of 120 to 150 words a minute, but our brains can process 400 to 800 words a minute.[1] Because we can process someone's words so quickly, we are tempted to begin thinking of other things. We may also become too focused on what we will say next in a conversation, and then we may interrupt the speaker before listening to the entire message. "Answering before listening is both stupid and rude" (Proverbs 18:13 MSG).

If we want to improve our listening skills, we should look at the life of Jesus. He was caring, compassionate, and considerate. He was not self-centered and egotistical. He truly listened to the needs of other people. Jesus said, "So pay attention to how you hear. To those who listen to my teaching, more understanding will be given. But for those who are not listening, even what they think they understand will be taken from them" (Luke 8:18 NLT).

When we yack less and listen more, we show other people a Christ-like consideration for their ideas. We become more empathetic and less apathetic. We can never truly understand people until we listen to what they have to say; then we may be able to show other people respect every day. To improve our listening skills, we must close our mouths and open our hearts; then we can truly communicate with other people.

We must listen to what people say,
And not let distractions get in the way.
If we truly want to know what is on someone's mind,
We must be quiet, courteous, and kind.
If we talk too much and engage in foolish chatter,
We make people think that they do not matter.
We should give others a chance to speak,
Because each person's ideas are special and unique.

YANK OUT THE WEEDS

"Then, after desire has conceived, it gives birth to sin; and sin, when it is full-grown, gives birth to death."

-James 1:15 (NIV)

$\mathcal{S}$in may appear to be harmless and attractive, but just like poisonous weeds in a garden, it must be yanked out! Some weeds produce beautiful flowers, but they are deadly! If you have any of these weeds in your garden, you need to yank them out!

- Jimson Weed—This plant produces a white bloom that looks like a morning glory flower, but the plant's seeds, roots, stems, and leaves are dangerous if ingested. Jimson weed is also called devil's snare.
- Meadow Death Camas—This plant has delicate blooms, and it is part of the lily family. All parts of the plant are toxic, including the bulb, which looks like a wild onion.
- Belladonna—The dark purple, bell-shaped flowers of this plant are pretty, but deadly. The leaves, fruits, and roots are highly toxic, whether eaten or just touched, especially if a person has an open wound. Belladonna is also known as deadly nightshade.
- Bittersweet Nightshade—This plant has pretty purple flowers and bright red berries, but the berries are poisonous to pets and can be deadly to children.

- Water Hemlock—This plant has lacy flowers and looks like wild carrots, but it is not edible. According to the USDA, water hemlock is the most toxic plant in North America.[1]

Sin grows like weeds in a garden. Just as some weeds have beautiful flowers, sin may appear harmless. But once sin takes root, it spreads like invasive weeds. The fastest-growing invasive weed in North America is kudzu, nicknamed the "foot-a-night vine" because it can literally grow a foot in a single day. It was imported from Japan in 1876, and it infests more than 7 million acres throughout the Southeast United States. It kills trees, destroys forests, pulls down power lines, and engulfs houses. Agronomists say it can take seven to ten years of repeated herbicide use and cutting and chopping to subdue an infestation of kudzu.[2]

Just like an invasive weed, sin can deeply take over a person's heart and mind, affecting thoughts, actions, and relationships. Some people think they can get away with sin, but they cannot fool God. "Do not be fooled: You cannot cheat God. People harvest only what they plant. If they plant to satisfy their sinful selves, their sinful selves will bring them ruin. But if they plant to please the Spirit, they will receive life from the Spirit" (Galatians 6:7-8 NCV).

If sin begins growing in your heart, you must yank it out so it will depart. If you allow sin to invade your life, it will become toxic and fill you with chaos and strife!

Sin is like an invasive weed;
It can penetrate a person's life with great speed.
Sin may appear harmless at first,
But when it takes hold, you are cursed.
Sin destroys your heart and soul,
And once it does, you are never whole.
So you must get rid of sin in your life,
Before it causes destruction and strife.

YOKE YOURSELF WITH JESUS

"Take my yoke upon you and learn from me, for I am gentle and humble in heart, and you will find rest for your souls. For my yoke is easy and my burden is light."

-Matthew 11:29-30 (NIV)

*A*nimals were often yoked together in biblical times to plow fields and pull wagons. A yoke is a wooden crosspiece fastened over the necks of two animals and attached to a plow or cart; the yoke allows the animals to share a load and pull together.

When we yoke ourselves with Jesus, He gives us rest from the burden of self-righteousness. The Pharisees in Jesus' day imposed heavy burdens upon the people with their legalistic law-keeping. According to biblical scholars, the Pharisees had added over 600 regulations regarding what constituted work on the Sabbath. Jesus said that any kind of law-keeping is a heavy burden. Jesus rebuked the Pharisees when He said, "They tie up heavy, cumbersome loads and put them on other people's shoulders, but they themselves are not willing to lift a finger to move them" (Matthew 23:4 NIV). No amount of law-keeping can save us. We are saved by faith—not by rituals and regulations! Faith does not impose a heavy weight upon us. Jesus carried the weight that we were meant to carry when He died on the cross. He took the burden of our sins with Him.

If we yoke ourselves to the world, we are in a constant state of strife. Imagine if two animals were unequally yoked together. They would end up fighting with each other. If we choose to yoke ourselves with non-Christians, we may end up compromising our faith. "Do not be yoked together with unbelievers. For what do righteousness and wickedness have in common? Or what fellowship can light have with darkness?" (2 Corinthians 6:14 NIV). A Christian pursuing God and a non-Christian pursuing the world will be pulling in different directions, so we should be careful whose yoke we accept.

Two animals equally yoked together are amazing! A Belgian draft horse can pull 8,000 pounds, so you would assume that when yoked with another Belgian draft horse, the two horses could pull 16,000 pounds; however, when the two are yoked together, they can pull up to 24,000 pounds. But when they are trained together, their pulling capacity increases to 32,000 pounds, which is astounding![1]

We must decide if we want to be yoked to life or death. If we are yoked to Jesus, we will have life; if we are yoked to sin, we will have death. We will become slaves to sin if we are not yoked to Jesus. "It is for freedom that Christ has set us free. Stand firm, then, and do not let yourselves be burdened again by a yoke of slavery" (Galatians 5:1 NIV). Christ freed us from the heavy burden of our sin when He died upon the cross. Because of His sacrifice, we are no longer tied to the yoke of slavery.

Yoke yourself with Jesus if you want rest;
You will find peace and be blessed.
If you yoke yourself with Jesus every day,
He will lighten your load along the way.
Jesus will carry what burdens your soul;
He will take the weight from you and make you whole.
Do you want to carry the yoke of sin's slavery,
Or yoke yourself with Jesus, who sets you free?

Z

Zap Your Bad Habits

"You were taught, with regard to your former way of life, to put off your old self, which is being corrupted by its deceitful desires; to be made new in the attitude of your minds; and to put on the new self, created to be like God in true righteousness and holiness."

– Ephesians 4:22-24 (NIV)

We all have habits, whether good or bad. As Christians, we are constantly being transformed by the renewal of our minds. Some of us may have the bad habit of lying to ourselves and to others. We are to put off our old nature and put on our new nature. This may take a lifetime. "Do not lie to each other. You have left your old, sinful life and the things you did before. You have begun to live the new life, in which you are being made new and are becoming like the one who made you. This new life brings you the true knowledge of God" (Colossians 3:9-10 NCV). This is not easy, and it is impossible if we only rely on our own strength.

Some of us have bad habits pertaining to our health. According to the CDC, more than one million people have died since 1999 from drug overdoses. We must remember that our bodies are temples. "Don't you realize that your body is the temple of the Holy

Spirit, who lives in you and was given to you by God? You do not belong to yourself, for God bought you with a high price. So you must honor God with your body" (1 Corinthians 6:19-20 NLT).

Some people have the bad habit of always being late! People who are habitually late for meetings, appointments, and events are unreliable and inconsiderate of other people's time. These people always make excuses for their tardiness, and they fail to realize the problems they cause because they are late! As followers of Christ, we should consider the effects of our tardiness on other people. "When you do things, do not let selfishness or pride be your guide. Instead, be humble and give more honor to others than to yourselves" (Philippians 2:3 NCV).

In order to overcome the bad habit of being late, people need to manage their time better. Rather than focusing on what time they need to be at their destination, they should plan what time they need to leave their house, allowing extra time for delays caused by trains, slow-moving vehicles, accidents, and weather conditions. Being prepared the night before an early morning departure is also helpful. Everything needed for the next day should be easily accessible; there is no reason to scurry around and look for necessary items at the last minute!

We should seek God's help in overcoming bad habits in our lives, and we should look for wisdom in replacing bad habits with good habits. We must stay connected to the one who can help us overcome our bad habits. "I am the vine; you are the branches. If you remain in me and I in you, you will bear much fruit; apart from me you can do nothing" (John 15:5 NIV).

If bad habits are causing problems in our lives, then we need to zap them before they get out of control!

When a bad habit is controlling your life,
It causes you to feel distress and strife.
The only way to zap the habit controlling you
Is to follow what Christ wants you to do.
If you listen to what His words say,
You can change your bad habits day by day.
If you think your bad habit will never disappear,
Just rely on Jesus, who is always near.

Zipline When You Can

"But those who hope in the Lord will renew their strength. They will soar on wings like eagles; they will run and not grow weary, they will walk and not be faint."

– Isaiah 40:31 (NIV)

If you have ever ziplined, you know the freedom you feel when soaring through the air! It feels like you are weightless, and the cares of the world do not weigh you down. Ziplining reduces stress, gives you an adrenaline rush, and boosts your self-confidence. Ziplining is for all ages. According to Guinness World Records, the oldest person to ever zipline was Jack Reynolds, who was 106 years old!

You can learn valuable life lessons from soaring through the air when you are ziplining.

- Freedom—You are free from the weight of the world when you are soaring through the air. You would not carry a heavy backpack with you or bring unnecessary equipment, so why do you carry the weight of the world with you every day when you could give your burdens to Christ? He will set you free! "So if the Son sets you free, you will be free indeed" (John 8:36 NIV).

- Courage—You must lay your fear aside and rely on the cables to support your weight when you zipline. Imagine how you might feel if you were on the highest zipline in the world. It is the La Tyrolienne, located in the French Alps on the Val Thorens ski resort. This zipline is at an altitude of 10,597 feet![1] The steepest zipline in the world is Zipflyer, in Nepal's Highgrounds Adventure Park. This zipline has a 2,000-foot vertical drop, and it reaches speeds up to 80 miles per hour.[2] If you rely on Christ each day, you will not have an attitude of fear. "God did not give us a spirit that makes us afraid but a spirit of power and love and self-control" (2 Timothy 1:7 NCV).

- Patience—You usually do not get the opportunity to zipline every day. Sometimes you must wait until you are vacationing or traveling to get this opportunity. Patience makes you slow down and wait. This is not what most people are accustomed to doing in our fast-paced society, but the benefits outweigh the time spent waiting. If you want to soar like an eagle, you may need to be patient. Sometimes eagles perch and wait for days for thermal updrafts to occur. These updrafts allow the eagles to soar and conserve their energy. The updrafts also enable eagles to soar high above storms. So, if you want to soar, you must wait upon the Lord. "Wait for the Lord; be strong and take heart and wait for the Lord" (Psalm 27:14 NIV).

If you want to soar on eagle's wings, try ziplining! You will feel free from the burdens of life as you glide through the air without any cares!

If you feel your burdens are weighing you down,
Try ziplining, and you will smile—not frown.
You will soar like an eagle as you glide
With freedom and courage by your side.
Your problems will disappear as you zip through the air
Without a worry or a care.
Remember that Christ wants you to be free of fear
And He is always with you and always near.

ZONE IN ON WHAT MATTERS MOST

"It is written, 'As surely as I live, says the Lord, every knee will bow before me; every tongue will acknowledge God.' So then, each of us will give an account of ourselves to God."

-Romans 14:11-12 (NIV)

*W*hat matters most to you? Is it prestige, power, and possessions? Is it trophies and treasures? None of these things will matter when you stand before God! The only thing that will matter is if you accepted Jesus as your Savior! Did you live a life following Christ or a life following the world? Did you follow Jesus' command to love others, or did you only love yourself?

- Accept Jesus as your Savior! "If you openly declare that Jesus is Lord and believe in your heart that God raised him from the dead, you will be saved" (Romans 10:9 NLT). You will experience joy and peace when Jesus saves you from your sins. This does not mean you will live a life of prosperity—you will have pain. What it does mean is that you will spend eternity in Heaven. Accepting Jesus as your Savior is the only way to Heaven—there is no other way.
- Keep pressing on! "Brothers and sisters, I do not consider myself yet to have taken hold of it. But one thing I do: For-

getting what is behind and straining toward what is ahead, I press on toward the goal to win the prize for which God has called me heavenward in Christ Jesus" (Philippians 3:13-14 NIV). Because our hope is in Christ, we can let go of past guilt and look forward to a more meaningful life. We should not take our eyes off the goal—knowing Christ and becoming like Him. Pressing toward the goal takes a lifetime of following Christ, and it requires determined endurance to stay the course throughout the trials, temptations, and travails of life; however, our eternal reward is worth it all!

- Love others! "Dear friends, since God so loved us, we also ought to love one another" (1 John 4:11 NIV). Loving other people requires the same sacrificial love with which God loves us. God loved us so much that He sacrificed Jesus to die on the cross for our sins. God loved us when we were unlovable. When we truly love others, we sacrifice our own selfish desires for other people. True love is a matter of the will—not our feelings.

Every knee will bow before God! Whether you are a peasant or a president, whether you live in a trailer or a townhouse, whether you are a beggar or a billionaire, you will kneel before God and give an account of your life. Your trophies and titles will not matter! Your money and material possessions will be worthless! When you kneel before God, you must be able to say that you accepted Jesus as your Savior, you kept pressing on, and you loved others.

So, if you want a life that is worthwhile and great, you must discover what matters most before it is too late!

What will matter most when you face your dying hour?
Will you seek comfort from your possessions and power?
Will you try to find contentment in your material things?
Hoping for the happiness each item brings?
Hopefully, you will realize before time runs out,
What matters most and what life is all about!

EPILOGUE

When life's problems are too heavy to bear,
And anxiety and fear are everywhere.
When discouragement eats away at your heart,
And doubt and despair will not depart.
When troubles tear you apart each day,
And turmoil and tragedy get in your way.
Then bid your burdens goodbye and let them go,
And you will find that your blessings will overflow!

Notes

Aim for Contentment

1. "Helen Lemmel." Last.fm. Accessed September 13, 2025. https://www.last.fm/music/Helen+Lemmel
2. "Turn Your Eyes Upon Jesus." *Hymnal.net*. Accessed September 13, 2025. https://www.hymnal.net

Avoid Temptations and Traps

1. "The Hunt for Forrest Fenn's Treasure." *CBS News*. May 25, 2024. https://www.cbsnews.com/pictures/forrest-fenn-treasure-hunt

Believe in the Goodness of God

1. "Karolina Wilhelmina Sandell-Berg." *Hymndex.com*. Accessed September 13, 2025. https://www.hymndex.com/karolina-wilhelmina-sandell-berg
2. "Joseph M. Scriven." *Hymndex.com*. Accessed September 13, 2025. https://www.hymndex.com/joseph-m-scriven

Brighten Someone's Day

1. "At the Front." Mount Vernon. Accessed September 15, 2025. https://www.mountvernon.org/george-washington/martha-washington/martha-at-the-front
2. "Mary Ann Bickerdyke." *Britannica*. Accessed September 15, 2025. https://www.britannica.com/biography/Mary-Ann-Bickerdyke

Build on a Firm Foundation

1. Ceballos, Joshua. "Surfside Condo Was Sinking for Years, and So Are Other Miami Structures, Says FIU Prof." *Miami New Times.* June 24, 2021. https://www.miaminewtimes. com/news/surfsides-champlain-towers-condo-was-sinking-fiu-researcher-says-12431246

2. Burke, Minyvonne. "Hiker Trapped in Quicksand in Utah for Hours Until Rescuers Could Reach and Free Him." *NBC News.* February 18, 2019. https://ww.nbcnews.com/news/ us-news/hiker-trapped-quicksand-utah-hours-until-rescuers-could-reach-free-n972836

Clear Away the Confusion

1. "Jim Bakker." *Britannica.* https://www.britannica.com/ biography/Jim-Bakker

Depart from Despair

1. Johnson, Zeta. "Living Without Hate—The Porter Halyburton Story." *Marines.* March 6, 2024. https://www.newriver. marines.mil/News/Article/Article/3697376/living-without-hate-the-porter-halyburton-story

2. Brotherton, Marcus. "Bataan Survivor, 101, Remembers Enduring POW Camps Because 'God Sustained Me.'" *Fox News.* January 7, 2023. https://www.foxnews.com/opinion/ bataan-survivor-101-remembers-enduring-pow-camps-because-god-sustained-me

Flee from Fear

1. "Perpetua." *Britannica.* https://www.britannica.com/biography/Perpetua-Christian-martyr

2. "St. Thomas Becket." *Britannica.* https://www.britannica. com/biography/Saint-Thomas-Becket

Forgive Others

1. Yardley, William. "Eric Lomax, World War II Prisoner Who Forgave, Dies at 93." *New York Times.* October 9, 2012. https://www.nytimes.com/2012/10/10/books/eric-lomax-river-kwai-prisoner-who-forgave-dies-at-93.html

Give More Than You Take

1. "Andrew Carnegie." *History.* February 9, 2021. https://www.history.com/topics/19th-century/andrew-carnegie

Hand Over the Remote Control

1. "Hymn History: 'I Surrender All.'" *Institute in Basic Life Principles.* https://www.iblp.org/hymn-history-i-surrender-all

Help Other People

1. Michals, Debra. "Clara Barton." *National Women's History Museum.* https://www.womenshistory.org/education-resources/biographies/clara-barton
2. *Samaritans Purse.* https://www.samaritanspurse.org/our-ministry/about-us

Hold on a Little Longer

1. Davey, Sally. "Just as I Am…' The Life of Charlotte Elliott." *Christian Library.* https://www.christianstudylibrary.org/article/just-i-am-...-life-charlotte-elliott
2. "Billy Graham's Life & Ministry by the Numbers." *Lifeway Research.* February 21, 2018. https://research.lifeway.com/2018/02/21/billy-grahams-life-ministry-by-the-numbers

Identify Your Invincibility

1. Koukos, Nikos. "3 People with Unimaginable Strength Who Saved Someone's Life." *Families.* https://vocal.media/

families/3-people-with-unimaginable-strength-who-saved-someone-s-life

2. "How Superhuman Strength Happens." *Healthline.* https://www.healthline.com/health/hysterical-strength

Imagine Your Amazing Future

1. Roeleveld, Lori Stanley. "10 Classic Hymns about Heaven." *Christianity.com.* June 10, 2022. https://www.christianity.com/wiki/christian-life/classic-inspiring-hymns-about-heaven.html

Lighten Your Load with Laughter

1. Tiret, Holly. "History of Humor and Health." *Michigan State University.* June 20, 2014. https://www.canr.msu.edu/news/history_of_humor_and_health

Modify Your Mindset

1. "Jim Jones." *Britannica.* https://www.britannica.com/biography/Jim-Jones

Move Forward—Not Backward

1. Bunyan, Roger. "Plennie Wingo." *Wired for Adventure.* March 22, 2022. https://www.wiredforadventure.com/article/plennie-wingo

Notice God's Magnificent Creation

1. "10 Great Big Yellowstone Facts." *Yellowstone Forever.* https://www.yellowstone.org/10-yellowstone-facts
2. "Folliott Sandford Pierpoint." *Hymnary.org.* https://www.hymnary.org/person/Pierpoint_FS
3. "For the Beauty of the Earth." *Hymnary.org.* https://www.hymnary.org/text/for_the_beauty_of_the_earth

Offer Kindness—Not Cruelty

1. "Dallmer, Mary [Mother Mary Joseph] (1852-1909)." *Texas State Historical Association*. https://tshaonline.org/handbook/entries/dallmer-mary-mother-mary-joseph
2. "Harold Godfrey Lowe." *Encyclopedia Titanica*. https://www.encyclopedia-titanica.org/titanic-survivor/harold-godfrey-lowe
3. "Oskar Schindler." *Britannica*. https://www.britannica.com/biography/Oskar-Schindler

Praise God in the Storms

1. Harland, Mike. "The Unknown Stories Behind Three Well-Loved Hymns." *Lifeway Research*. June 25, 2018. https://research.lifeway.com/2018/06/25/the-unknown-backstories-to-3-well-loved-hymns
2. "It Is Well with My Soul." *Hymnary.org*. https://www.hymnary.org/text/when_peace_like_a_river_attendeth_my_way

Pray More—Panic Less

1. Mark, Joshua J. "William Tyndale." *World History Encyclopedia*. April 2, 2022. https://www.worldhistory.org/William_Tyndale
2. "The Inspiring Life of George Müller." *Guideposts*. https://guideposts.org/inspiring-stories/the-inspiring-life-of-george-muller

Quell the Quarrels in Your Life

1. "Hatfields and McCoys." *Britannica*. https://www.britannica.com/topic/Hatfields-and-McCoys

Quit Your Quest for More Stuff

1. "Imelda Marcos." *Biography*. May 10, 2021. https://www.biography.com/political-figures/imelda-marcos

2. O'Connor, Maureen. "5 Shopping Sprees So Wild, They Made History." *The Cut.* April 15, 2013. https://www.thecut.com/2013/04/5-shopping-sprees-so-wild-they-made-history.html

Run Your Own Race

1. Taylor, Bill. "What Breaking the 4-Minute Mile Taught Us About the Limits of Conventional Thinking." *Harvard Business Review.* March 9, 2018. https://www.hbr.org/2018/03/what-breaking-the-4-minute-mile-taught-us-about-the-limits-of-conventional-thinking
2. Mackay, Duncan. "Roger Bannister Beats John Landy in the 'Miracle Mile' at Vancouver 1954." *Inside the Games.* April 11, 2018. https://www.insidethegames.biz/articles/1063797/roger-bannister-beats-john-landy-in-the-miracle-mile-at-vancouver-1954

Seek Wisdom—Not Wealth

1. Robehmed, Natalie. "The Vanderbilts: How American Royalty Lost Their Crown Jewels." *Forbes.* June 17, 2019. https://www.forbes.com/sites/natalierobehmed/2014/07/14/the-vanderbilts-how-american-royalty-lost-their-crown-jewels

Stop Following the Wrong Path

1. Moye, Jayme. "Day Hikers Are the Most Vulnerable in Survival Situations. Here's Why." *National Geographic.* April 11, 2019. https://www.nationalgeographic.com/adventure/article/hikers-survival-tips

Unplug Every Day

1. "What to Know About Social Media Addiction." *Medical News Today.* https://www.medicalnewstoday.com/articles/social-media-addiction

Vitalize Your Faith

1. Klein, Christopher. "The Real-Life Olympic History Behind 'Chariots of Fire.'" *History.* August 5, 2024. https://www.history.com/news/chariots-of-fire-liddell-abrahams-1924-paris-olympics
2. "Fanny Crosby." *Britannica.* https://www.britannica.com/biography/Fanny-Crosby

Walk Away from Your Worries

1. "Corrie ten Boom." *Biography.* August 1, 2023. https://www.biography.com/articles/corrie-ten-boom

Work Wholeheartedly

1. "History of the Salvation Army." *Salvation Army.* https://www.salvationarmyusa.org/usn/history-of-the-salvation-army
2. *Billy Graham Evangelistic Association.* https://www.billygraham.org

X-irradiate the Darkness

1. "Joan of Arc." *History.* July 13, 2022. https://www.history.com/topics/middle-ages/saint-joan-of-arc
2. "Saint Francis of Assisi." *Biography.* April 21, 2021. https://www.biography.com/religious-figures/saint-francis-of-assisi

X-out the Stain of Sin

1. "Nothing But the Blood of Jesus." *Hymnary.org.* https://www.hymnary.org/text/what_can_wash_away_my_sin

Yack Less—Listen More

1. Lucas, Stephen E. *The Art of Public Speaking.* 11th ed. New York: McGraw-Hill, 2012.

Yank Out the Weeds

1. Locker, Melissa. "These Are the Most Dangerous Flowering Weeds That May Be in Your Yard." *Southern Living.* May 10, 2023. https://www.southernliving.com/garden/flowers/poisonous-weeds-with-flowers
2. Schleicher, Jerry. "The Worst Invasive Plants and Garden Weeds." *Grit Rural Farm Know-How.* April 18, 2011. https://www.grit.com/farm-and-garden/invasive-plants-garden-weeds

Yoke Yourself with Jesus

1. Lund, John B. "The Power of Pulling Together." *America First Newsroom.* https://news.americafirst.com/the-power-of-pulling-together

Zipline When You Can

1. "Tyrolienne in French Alps, the Highest Zipline in the World." Minikin Escapades. https://www.minikinescapades.com/highest-zipline-la-tyrolienne/
2. "ZipFlyer Nepal. The World's Steepest Zipline." Highground Adventures. https://www.highgroundnepal.com/zipflyer